THE WHOLE
CHRISTIAN

THE WHOLE CHRISTIAN

Elizabeth R. Skoglund

1817

HARPER & ROW, PUBLISHERS
New York, Hagerstown, San Francisco, London

FIRST EDITION

Designed by Janice Stern

Library of Congress Cataloging in Publication Data

Skoglund, Elizabeth.
   The whole Christian.
     1. Christianity—Psychology. I. Title.
BR110.S54   1976   201'.1'9   75-12288
ISBN 0-06-067391-5

76 77 78 79 10 9 8 7 6 5 4 3 2 1

To Bob and Anne Pedrick

Contents

Preface

Years ago when my aunt returned to the United States from missionary work in China and Formosa, she was broken in body from bad nutrition and the ravages of typhus, and she seemed mentally dislocated and disoriented in a country which had changed many times in her absence. As a young adult I felt that if she just could claim God's promises she would feel fine again. I was not trying to be cruel nor was I lacking in compassion, for it was an honest belief. And in spite of that belief, I tried in every way I knew to help her. Yet deep down I really believed that she wasn't adequately trusting God.

Then a number of circumstances made me reevaluate my narrow position. I noticed that people who spiritualized all their problems didn't always seem able to put that theory to practical use when faced with a crisis. *Reality Therapy* by William Glasser, M.D., opened my mind affirmatively to the possibilities of good psychotherapy. My work with drug users made me begin to realize that while they were in spiritual need, often that was not their only need—nor was their only need psychological. My thinking with regard to emotional problems expanded to include the physical dimension as well as the spiritual and psychological. From that time on, my counseling with people of all ages has seemed to confirm man's need in all three areas and has shown me that good medicine, sound counseling, and real Christianity are not contradictory or damaging to each other. To the contrary, they are complementary.

I am grateful to Bob and Anne Pedrick for their encouragement in perceiving the balance between these areas and for enabling me to sort out my thinking. With their help, rather than becoming embittered against the narrowness of certain branches of Christianity, I have been able to develop a vital faith in God which is not threatened or tarnished by accepting myself as a three-part being. My gratitude is directed once again toward Glenn Wiest for being my best teacher and example as a therapist and toward Calvin Elrod, M.D., Harvey Ross, M.D., and Granville Knight, M.D., for their medical advice and instruction. All four of these men stand at the top of their fields; yet each gave me much time during the writing of the book in reading incomplete manuscript pages and in both criticizing and encouraging any ideas while never forcing change.

I appreciate my mother who reads everything I ever write before anyone else sees it and Lee Petty who is always pushing me into the next book before I've finished the last.

Last, I am indebted to Janet Camp for her perfection and dependability in typing and to Linda and Charlotte Griffin and Irene Correia for filling in on that typing.

Foreword

In reading the manuscript of *The Whole Christian*, I was reminded of my own career as a counselor. Part way through my training I began to suspect that counseling did not always work—a conclusion that was very threatening to me as a neophyte psychologist. When I began reading about research in psychotherapy, my insecurities about counseling increased even more and at the time of my completing graduate school I felt less than enthusiastic about my chosen career. Imagine—a Ph.D. in clinical psychology who was not sure how to counsel and was not even convinced that counseling did any good.

Then, a few years later, I met Paul Tournier and things began to change. When he was thirty-eight the doctor, who had become a Christian as a child, gave himself completely to Christ and began to see radical changes in his life and work. A Christianity which had been ritualistic and cold became vibrant and meaningful. Patients who had previously been treated as "disease entities" suddenly became persons in need of love and attention. An aloof medical manner gave way to a warm concern and caring for others. Before long Tournier began to recognize that his fellow human beings were "whole persons"—with physical bodies, spiritual needs, and psychological characteristics. To treat one part of the personality while ignoring the other parts was, Tournier concluded, bad medicine and unbalanced Christianity. Before long Tournier was talking about the "medicine of the whole person" and writing about "whole persons" in a broken world.

Soon it became clear why I had lost my faith in counseling: I had overemphasized counseling techniques, important as these are, and had neglected the ingredients of love, compassion, and concern on the part of the counselor. I had focused on the psychological characteristics of my counselees but largely overlooked their physical needs, their spiritual concerns, and their hunger for an intimate relationship with other human beings.

To grow as whole Christians and to help others in this growth is surely the task of every believer. It is this concern for wholeness which impressed me about Tournier; it is the same concern which is found in the pages of Elizabeth Skoglund's *The Whole Christian*.

Elizabeth Skoglund has written a volume to help all of us in this growth process. She is a person who has discovered the meaning of wholeness in the Christian life and with clarity and great human interest has shared her discovery with others. Unique to this volume is the inclusion of some of the newest advances in the field of orthomolecular medicine, which involves the replacement into the body of deficiencies such as vitamins and minerals. Along with the insights in the metabolic area there is an equally consistent psychological and spiritual emphasis. According to the author, Biblical Christianity, sound psychology, and innovative medicine are not contradictory but rather complement one another.

In *The Whole Christian* the author draws on a wealth of counseling experiences to clarify her conclusions, and her deep compassion for others shines forth. I like her thesis—that the truly balanced Christian life must include physical and psychological as well as spiritual well-being. This is a book which can be helpful to laymen and to counselors alike. Christians who have failed in their quest for wholeness by neglecting the total person will obtain new insights in the reading of this book. It is an optimistic work with an important message—that each of us can and should become whole Christians.

GARY R. COLLINS

Trinity Evangelical Divinity School
Deerfield, Illinois

THE WHOLE
CHRISTIAN

CHAPTER 1

The Whole Christian

"Just go home and get more sleep. You students stay up too late."

With that advice, based purely on the intuition of the intern consulted, Janelle walked slowly out of the university clinic and back to her dorm. It was Janelle's last year of college, and she had just turned twenty-one. In recent weeks her fatigue had become almost intolerable. During the past few days she had felt a rather intense depression.

Although Janelle's childhood had been anything but ideal, until now she had seemed to escape with few psychological scars; physically she had always been quite healthy.

Now as she walked along, the "just go home and get more sleep" advice didn't seem worth the effort she had made to go to the clinic. Sleep! That's all she seemed to do these days. Yet he was a doctor, if only an intern. Confused, Janelle decided that she would have to endure her symptoms a while longer and hope they would go away.

As the remaining months of the school semester went by, Janelle got steadily worse and dropped several classes in order to keep going. A feeling of desperation set in. What if she never got better?

Her boyfriend, who usually understood her, began to wonder if their proposed marriage would really work. Janelle wondered too. How could she develop a good marital relationship when she was so tired and depressed that she could hardly make it to her next class?

About this time the people in her church where she was a

very active member began to give bits of advice. Many affirmed her and suggested doctors or offered constructive counsel; others, however, were critical. "Why don't you ask God to show you where you're sinning?" suggested one middle-aged lady who had never been sick a day in her life and attributed her good health to God's reward for moral living. Some others didn't feel that God was punishing Janelle for sin, but they did try to impress upon her the need to improve the quality of her spiritual life since, according to them, God "never allows depression in the life of a Christian"—unless, of course, that Christian isn't spiritual enough.

By now Janelle had been sick for about eight months. She had broken her engagement and felt worthless both spiritually and psychologically. Then in the middle of all the bad advice, one insightful person suggested that she go to a physician who had helped several friends of hers. As a last resort, Janelle made the appointment.

But the Janelle who sat in that doctor's office was not the same calm, logical college student who had gone to the university clinic months before. She was defensive, nervous, and, in general, negative about everything. The bad psychological climate of her childhood had begun to manifest itself in a lack of a sense of self-worth, a state which her well-meaning Christian friends had cultivated. Above all was the constant, nagging fatigue.

Wisely, the physician didn't make a quick diagnosis based on surface observations. Rather, he gave her a thorough physical examination and ran a large battery of tests. The diagnosis? Rather simple but devastating if ignored. Janelle had a very low-functioning thyroid which was aggravating the fatigue, depression, and even the anxiety.

But because human beings are complex mechanisms, medical treatment alone was not the solution to Janelle's problem. The amount of time that elapsed before she was correctly diagnosed had caused a breakdown in some of the defenses she had built around her unhappy childhood; and so feelings of inferiority had been intensified. Since any chronic illness can make a person feel weak and inadequate, Janelle's physical problem in itself affected her self-image. In addition, a low thyroid condition directly causes weakness and depression. When you add to all these complications, the broken engagement and the spiritual putdown, it becomes obvious that Janelle's physician would have a hard time knowing where the physical, psychological, and spiritual aspects of Janelle's problem each began and ended. It took medication, psychotherapy, and positive spiritual counseling to help Janelle back to a normal life.

Convenient as it may be to compartmentalize a human being and say, "This problem is all spiritual or all psychological or all physical," such an attitude is simplistic and can increase a person's difficulties. While people are made up of all of these components, each interrelates with the other until they often become blurred and indistinguishable one from the other.

In "The American Scholar" Ralph Waldo Emerson discusses the paradox of the whole having several parts and yet being one.

It is one of those fables which out of an unknown antiquity convey an unlooked-for wisdom, that the gods, in the beginning, divided Man into men, that he might be more helpful to himself; just as the hand was divided into fingers, the better to answer its end.

The old fable covers a doctrine ever new and sublime; that there is One Man—present to all particular men only partially, or through one faculty; and that you must take the whole society to find the whole man. Man is not a farmer, or a professor, or an engineer, but he is all. Man is priest, and scholar, and statesman, and producer, and soldier.[1]

To take Emerson's idea one step further, any individual is not divided neatly into three parts but is a total of all three. A loaf of bread is made up of several ingredients such as flour and eggs and milk. Each is distinct from the others, but once they are combined into a loaf of bread, they cease to be distinct and separate. Instead of being eggs, flour, and milk, they become bread. Likewise a person is not three equal parts—body, mind, and spirit—but a whole made up of all three. Yet, in spite of this interrelationship, at times one part may stand out from the others, and here the loaf of bread analogy stops.

A sixteen-year-old with a drug problem came to my office. In the course of our counseling sessions she became a Christian. The psychological effect was profound. Instead of floundering around, without friends or purpose, she began to fill her life with meaningful activities and, eventually, healthy relationships. Christianity greatly affected the progress she made in counseling. In her, the spirit had been most neglected.

Suzanne, a Christian in her late forties, had a very low regard for herself and some psychosomatic problems as well. Counseling consisted partially of convincing her that she did not have to feel "sinful" because she had some emotional problems. Once over that hurdle, she responded more quickly than some in developing greater self-esteem. Her stomach problems disappeared, and it became easier for her to relate to God when the neurotic guilt was gone.

Michael, in contrast to the other two, was an eleven-year-old child who had suffered from a variety of rather serious illnesses all his life. His low self-esteem seemed very tied in to the fact that he was a always sick. His sickness made him feel weak and inadequate. He would say things like, "I'm just a bother to my parents. They have to stay home all the time." Progress in counseling was slow. Just about the time he really began to improve, Mike would get sick, and the cycle would start all over again.

A person's body, mind, and spirit make up a totality in which one or the other may emerge predominantly at any given time. A woman going through the menopause may experience periods of depression which should not be labeled as primarily psychological or spiritual. She may derive help from spiritual or psychological sources, but the primary cause is physical. Certain drugs are now being used effectively with some forms of mental illness, further validating the biochemical basis for many emotional problems.

It has also been shown that stress produces its own set of

physical responses. Fatigue can point to an underlying state of depression. Stress can cause a myriad of metabolic imbalances. A young girl I once knew produced asthma symptoms every time she became emotionally upset. Another developed a rash which would leave immediately after the stressful situation was resolved.

A person's spiritual life too may be directly affected by his physical and emotional state. It is often more difficult to feel spiritually strong when you feel physically or psychologically weak. Esau sold his birthright, not when he was physically strong, but when he was exhausted and hungry. Peter denied Christ under the duress of a young girl's mockery.

The idea that we are a composite of body, mind, and spirit is not new by any means. The Bible says that "A cheerful heart does good like medicine" (Prov. 17:22), implying a relationship between the body and the mind. In Proverbs 15:30 we read, "Pleasant sights and good reports give happiness and health." "Hope deferred makes the heart sick" (Prov. 13:12). "Reverence for God gives a man deep strength" (Prov. 14:26).

More recently than biblical times and yet almost a century ago, Charles H. Spurgeon, a man still well known and esteemed for his godliness, preached a remarkable sermon. He said:

> It is not necessary to prove by quotations from the biographies of eminent ministers that seasons of fearful prostration have fallen to the lot of most if not all of them. The life of Luther might suffice to give a thousand instances and he was by no means of the weakest sort. His great spirit was often in the seventh heaven of exultation, and as frequently on the borders of despair.[2]

As to the reason for such despair, Spurgeon goes on to relate the mind, body, and spirit:

> Certain bodily maladies are fruitful fountains of despondency. And let a man strive as he may against their influence, there will be hours and circumstances in which they will overcome him.

As for mental maladies, is any man altogether sane? Are we not all a little off balance? Some minds appear to have a gloomy tinge essential to their individuality. . . .

These infirmities may be no detriment to a man's career of usefulness. They may even have been imposed upon him by divine wisdom as a necessary qualification for his peculiar course of service . . .[3]

Then, rather than overspiritualizing emotional problems and denying that Christians should ever have any, Spurgeon continues in quite an opposite view:

But where in body and mind there are predisposing causes to lowness of spirit, it is no marvel if in dark moments the heart succumbs to them. The wonder in many cases is—and if inner lives could be written, men would see it so—how some keep at their work at all and still wear a smile upon their countenance. Grace has its triumphs and patience its martyrs, martyrs none the less to be honored because flames kindle about their spirits rather than their bodies, and their burning is unseen by human eyes . . .[4]

Without question there can be any number of psychological causes for the emotional problems which confront people. However, both the cause and the cure should not in many cases be disconnected from the physical and the spiritual. More important for Christians to realize is that, while help in handling emotional problems will certainly be found in a relationship with Christ, the complete answer may not be spiritual at all. This realization will save many a Christian from feeling guilt over his or her emotional problems and will prevent some Christians from sinning by self-righteous judgment of others.

There is a peculiarly unchristian or perhaps I should say pseudo-Christian attitude present in Christian circles today which condemns a Christian who has emotional problems. "Christian Counseling: Who Has the Answer?" by Vernon Grounds and Gary Collins appeared in *Eternity* not long ago and gave a good, objective overview of the scene. In it Jay

Adams, a minister *not* a psychotherapist, is quoted as feeling that "psychotherapy is the biggest deception since Jacob tricked Esau. . . . He asserts that emotional difficulties are caused by sinful behavior and attitudes, and that the correct prescription for handling all such problems is to be found in the Bible, or at least must be prayerfully developed in harmony with Biblical objectives." Furthermore, says Collins, "Adams argues that the ordained pastor (not the psychologist) is the only person who is really competent to counsel . . ." Moreover, Adams is quoted by Collins as having some interesting but destructive notions such as: "Behavior always precedes feelings; problems can have only three causes; sin, organic disorder or demon activity."[5]

In further reading and in talking to other professionals as well as patients, I am appalled by many of the distorted ideas relating to psychological problems and counseling which exist in some Christian thinking. If Christians are to benefit from psychological help, some of these misconceptions must be discussed in depth and resolved. Certain Christians actually view counseling as something which should be totally spiritual; they seem to ignore the psychological dimension all together. The resultant denigration of non-Christian therapists is unfair and does nothing to promote the concept of the love of Christ, for often non-Christian therapists are viewed almost as agents of Satan, waiting to seduce the Christian who comes to them.[6] One man is actually quoted as having said: ". . . if his patients would not accept Jesus Christ, he could not help them."[7]

There are really two problems here: the inability to see emotional problems apart from spiritual problems, and the mistaken idea that all Christian therapists promote spirituality in their patients and that all non-Christian therapists attempt to destroy their patients' Christianity. From my own acquaintance with psychotherapists, the good ones do not try to discourage their patients' Christian beliefs. Furthermore, while a competent Christian therapist is certainly ideal for a Christian who has problems, I have run into a number of so-called Christian therapists who are confused spiritually and not very proficient psychologically. Although many people, Christian and non-

Christian, have had some deplorable experiences with psycho-therapists, from what I hear in my office, that experience has been true of both Christian *and* non-Christian therapists. There are more non-Christian therapists than Christian, and many of them are very effective, just as are unbelieving lawyers, doctors, and plumbers.

Some Christians also seem to feel that Christian therapists are the only ones who demand a sense of responsibility from a person, hence again the need for a Christian counselor who will not downgrade their standards. Inherent here again is the idea that low standards and sin are at the root of most emotional problems.[8] Such a view of therapy which does not involve Christian counseling is based more on some older forms of psychoanalysis and on a few of the present far-out therapies which are on the fringes of more responsible therapy. In contrast, responsibility is greatly emphasized by psychiatrist William Glasser. For Christians to avoid the extremes of *some* forms of psychotherapy which do not demand responsibility from the patient by going to an opposite extreme and blaming emotional problems on sin is, in my opinion, equally irresponsible.

I question also the view of some Christians that communication should be totally open, that everything should be confessed in front of all parties involved.[9] Some things are better not said in front of one's wife or child. There is room for privacy in the counseling session. Indeed, is not part of the value of good counseling dependent on privacy and trust? When confession to a wife or a husband can only destroy the other person and is done, not out of moral need but out of the need to relieve oneself of guilt, then I believe the therapist's role is to help the person with his guilt rather than to encourage the confession. Many marriages have been destroyed because a husband confessed a single act of unfaithfulness in order to relieve his guilt and then found that his wife couldn't handle it. When this is done in the name of Christianity, one wonders what theological base is used to justify it.

Some Christians also have strong religious opinions[10] about specific emotional disorders which should never be spiritualized.

Manic-depression is one such area. Yet according to Harvey Ross, M.D., an orthomolecular psychiatrist in the Los Angeles area, manic-depressiveness is basically a biochemical disorder. The fact that the drug Lithium usually will remove symptoms in manic-depressives is proof of its organic basis. To spiritualize a problem which is basically organic is destructive since when the spiritual does not remove the problem then the patient can only feel profound guilt and defeat over his failure.

Something of the same type of spiritualization is true of homosexuality. InterVarsity Press and *Eternity* magazine have both published works which deal with this problem in a fair and compassionate manner. Yet many Christians still feel that the homosexual desire as well as the act are sinful. They imply that a complete cure is possible with spiritual help.[11] To the contrary, while according to the Bible the homosexual act is sinful, I find it hard to believe that a homosexual who may have begun to develop a distorted sexual self-image at as young an age as two is sinning because he feels homosexual impulses. His rejection of those impulses may make him a greater saint than a person with less temptation.

The potential for guilt and despair in many of these ideas disturbs me deeply. Talk about pushing someone when he or she is already down! Since a person with emotional problems usually has low self-esteem, you can imagine what happens to that self-esteem when he has to blame his problems on sin or demon activity, unless he's lucky enough to have a recognizable organic problem! (I have found that organic problems are not usually spiritualized.) The results of overspiritualizing can be quite crippling; and it is the most conscientious person, who has probably been more sinned against than sinful, who will be the most hurt.

Basic to all the problems that have been raised this far is the idea that negative emotions such as anger, fear and depression are always sinful.[12] From a biblical point of view this does not seem reasonable. David was frequently depressed, but I do not recall that he was condemned for that depression. Christ was repeatedly angry at the Pharisees. He showed deep fear and depression in the Garden of Gethsemane as he faced crucifixion.

His prayer was an agonizing plea for help. A misuse of anger or a groveling in depression and self-pity is both psychologically and spiritually damaging. But we all experience legitimate and nonsinful negative emotion. What we do with those emotions is the important thing, and sometimes seeking professional help is a positive, right reaction.

Many Christians seem to think that they are always to be the opposite of depressed, that is, happy and joyful. The rightness or wrongness of that viewpoint lies in one's definition of those words. A light sort of continued "up" feeling is not, in my opinion, what God expects of us; and to teach that this is a necessary characteristic of a good Christian is to cause great discouragement and guilt. What God does give to a Christian is a settled sense of contentment. One person who has suffered greatly said with tears: "I am glad that God has used my pain to bring something good into this world, and if I could choose to change it all and lose the good, I would not change even the pain. But I did not like the pain nor do I like it now." She was content but not masochistically happy over suffering. At times she had been depressed and frightened, but never had she lost that deep sense of God's control and strength in her life. Such an attitude reminds one of Paul's words: "We are troubled on every side, yet not distressed; we are perplexed, but not in despair; persecuted, but not forsaken; cast down, but not destroyed" (2 Cor. 4:8–9, KJV). Such are the words of true Christian balance, and they comfort the Christian who feels "unchristian" because he doesn't walk around in a continual "high."

C. S. Lewis in *The Problem of Pain* expresses Christian balance when he says:

When I think of pain—of anxiety that gnaws like fire and loneliness that spreads out like a desert, and the heartbreaking routine of monotonous misery, or again of dull aches that blacken our whole landscape or sudden nauseating pains that knock a man's heart out at one blow, of pains that seem already intolerable and then are suddenly increased, of infuriating scorpion-stinging pains that startle into maniacal movement a man who seemed half dead with his previous tortures—it quite o'ercrows my spirit. If I knew any way of escape I would crawl through sewers to find it. But what is the good of telling you about my feelings? You know them already: they are the same as yours. I am not arguing that pain is not painful. Pain hurts. That is what the word means. I am only trying to show that the old Christian doctrine of being made "perfect through suffering" is not incredible. To prove it palatable is beyond my design . . .[13]

Christians do not escape pain, but they do have added help in handling it when it comes.

There are, of course, others like Paul Tournier who have a much broader viewpoint than some pastoral counselors and Christian psychotherapists who are so vocal today. Unfortunately, however, those who have an overspiritualizing attitude toward emotional problems can, in my opinion, have a destructive effect on many. One man I know was for the first time in his whole life getting effective psychological help, in this case from group therapy. Then he read a book telling him that all emotional problems arose from sin; he began to feel guilty about his therapy and quit. His wife and children, who for the first time had seen him function appropriately as a husband and father, were bitterly disappointed—and angry at the author of that book, a man whom they had never met.

In my own practice I had a man suffer a setback in counseling when he read a popular book on depression. While some of the book's positive biblical teaching helped my patient, other statements made him feel guilty for ever being depressed in the first place. How ironic that an old-fashioned preacher like Spurgeon should be so much more liberal and compassionate! Sometimes I wonder what these extremists would do if they saw a five-year-old who tried to kill herself or a three-year-old schizophrenic staring blankly into space. Have they sinned too? I would ask. Is this demon activity or organic disease? What would they say, I wonder, to a five-year-old boy in an acute state of depression after witnessing his mother's death from an overdose of heroin?

A man in his late thirties who walks very closely with God recently saw me for a number of sessions because of his anxiety. At the end he said: "My minister told me not to seek psychological help because I should handle my problems spiritually. Now I feel better psychologically and spiritually, and I regret the ten years it took me to finally go to a counselor."

Counseling for emotional needs, like medical treatment for physical needs, is a God-given opportunity which Christians are meant to use. To seek counseling as well as to seek medical help does not imply a lack of trust in God. All three can work together toward making an individual a more complete, usable instrument of God.

NOTES

1. Ralph Waldo Emerson, "The American Scholar," *American Heritage*, ed. Leon Howard, Louis B. Wright, and Carl Brode Boston: D. C. Heath and Co., 1955), 1: 621.

2. Charles H. Spurgeon, "Discouragement," *His*, February 1962, p. 8.

3. Ibid., p. 9.

4. Ibid.

5. Vernon Grounds and Gary Collins, "Christian Counseling: Who Has the Answer?" *Eternity*, January 1975, pp. 16, 20.

6. Jay E. Adams, *The Christian Counselor's Manual* (Nutley, N.J.: Presbyterian and Reformed Publishing Co., 1973), p. 117.

7. Grounds and Collins, "Christian Counseling," pp. 18, 20.

8. Adams, *Christian Counselor's Manual*, p. 136.

9. Ibid., p. 269.

10. Ibid., p. 380.

11. Ibid., pp. 404–6.

12. Grounds and Collins, "Christian Counseling," pp. 18, 20.

13. C. S. Lewis, *The Problem of Pain* (New York: Macmillan, 1962), p. 105.

CHAPTER 2

———— • ————

The Body and Its Effect
on the Mind

When I was a counselor in a large high school, I became deeply involved in working with teenagers who were on drugs. I became intensely aware of the body's powers and of the power of chemicals introduced into that body, on the mind.

One particular day I kept noticing a boy whom I knew quite well following me cautiously at a distance. He looked distressed and yet seemed afraid to approach me. That was out of character for him. He was the type to interrupt me in the middle of a conference if he really needed me. Yet, not wanting to intrude myself upon him, I waited.

Around lunchtime, he slowly walked closer and closer to me. "I dropped a tab of acid [LSD] this morning," he said, "and I've never had such a bad trip. I'm afraid, even of you, and yet I feel safer if I'm near you."

We walked into a quiet room since noises were bothering him. Using a calm tone of voice I tried to reassure him that he would be okay. That helped, but the fear of people and noises was still written all over his face. Yet, with my support and the help of an understanding vice-principal, the boy got through the day without being thrown into a completely paranoid state. That night he called to say, "Thanks, I'm all right now! I thought you should know." He was calm and normal again.

I suppose that no one knows exactly how LSD works in the body, except that it acts as a catalyst which precipitates symptoms and reactions that may go on for hours or even days. Some people have flashbacks which repeat part of the LSD experience for a long time after they take the original pill.

During the years that I was with the schools, and somewhat since then, I have seen seemingly normal people become frightened, belligerent, euphoric, depressed, angry, aggressive, and apathetic as the result of taking a chemical. Of course, the drugs joined together with their personalities and with their existing problems, but without the drugs, the reactions would not have occurred.

The capacity of drugs to effect behavioral changes in human beings is obvious and readily accepted. However, the average person is not as aware of the body's affect on the emotions, apart from a drug.

A while back I talked late into the evening with a college student who was contemplating suicide. Joyce was a chemistry major in the university and was getting almost straight A's.

Both parents were alcoholics, too occupied with their own problems to care what happened to her. As a result, Joyce worked long hours in order to support herself while maintaining a full-time academic program.

For breakfast she had nothing but coffee, her other meals consisted of high-starch foods, and she slept only four hours a night. Her self-image, already not very sturdy due to a traumatic childhood, plummeted, and Joyce became desperate enough to want to escape life altogether. The factor that had finally made the difference was the physical stress on her body, for she improved rapidly with added sleep and good nutrition. Her capacity for a sense of relatedness to God was even improved by the positive changes in her body. When she was at a point of complete exhaustion, she felt that God was remote and that she did not have the energy to reach out to him. All she could do was passively trust. After her body was restored to better health, she felt an active involvement with God.

The longer I have been in the counseling profession, the more I have become aware that people's problems are frequently *not* all psychological or all spiritual—or even the two combined. To the contrary, the body plays an influential role in human emotions. Even traditional medical opinion supports this view to a limited degree although there is a tendency among some in the medical profession to psychologize all that they do not understand. Nor is this viewpoint limited to the medical profession alone. A well-known and generally broad-minded clergyman stated: "All of us have basically the same glands—it's what you put into them that makes the difference." While there is a basic truth in that statement, in that our psychological input *does* affect our bodies, the viewpoint that we all have the same glands is simplistic and ignores the tremendous influence of the body on the mind.

Any chronic illness has a definite effect on the psychological and spiritual aspects of a person. According to Calvin Elrod, M.D, a man in general practice who sees a great variety of patients, "Any serious but not terminal illness often causes a bad mental outlook."

One woman who was frequently hospitalized and consistently weak felt that her husband should no longer want her because she couldn't do a lot of things for him such as cooking, heavy housekeeping, and running frequent errands. Her physical weakness and her inability to do the many tasks often given to a wife made her feel a lessened sense of worth.

A college student who suffered from a chronic blood disorder couldn't travel much because of her potential need for immediate medical attention and was unable to perform ordinary functions such as driving, walking distances, or staying out late at parties. She felt different, in a sense, isolated from the world. She felt old before she was old. She once said to me: "Sometimes I get up in the morning and feel unusually well and strong. Then the day becomes easy, almost automatic. And I look around me and want to tell everyone how wonderful it feels to be able to have a day like this. But then I know that people wouldn't understand because this is just an average kind of day for them."

Many people who are chronically ill experience low self-esteem because they feel weak, inadequate, different. There is often the feeling that "I cannot cope with my responsibilities" or "I can't compete" or "I can't do what other people do," therefore "I am not a very worthwhile person."

While such feelings can be at least partially resolved, such a reaction is normal enough, for an abnormal reaction to an abnormal situation is normal. A man in combat on a battlefield will normally feel fear. A woman about to be attacked on a lonely, dark street will feel an appropriate sense of panic. Depression and grief are normal reactions to a death or a great loss of some kind. The abnormal person, someone out of contact with reality, would experience no negative feelings in such situations.

Sometimes we in the helping professions forget this. A young man who had been ill for a number of years with a misdiagnosis and therefore wrong treatment ended up in another physician's where he received a correct diagnosis. By this time, however, he had developed all sorts of emotional problems as a result of the frustrations caused by his illness. The doctor involved resisted the temptation to label the whole thing psychological and probed until he found the basic physical cause. Then with real empathy he said to the man, "You have emotional problems that need psychological help, but these problems would be expected after what you've been through." The man's situation was abnormal and thus the resultant emotional reactions.

Conversely, a young girl was hospitalized because she wanted to withdraw from barbiturate addiction. As the drugs were taken away, the symptoms started, emotional as well as physical. Her attitude, however, was one of determination. Early one morning she was lying in bed crying out of physical agony as well as out of fear and loneliness. Her doctor happened to walk in and in a tone of partial disgust said: "What are you crying for? I didn't think you were that kind of person." Her feelings of pain were only intensified by his rejection of them.

To react against pain is appropriate. Thus, for the chronically ill person to feel a sense of inadequacy and alienation is probably normal and is certainly not something to be ashamed of.

However, realizing that one's self-worth is attacked in a chronic illness may be a first step toward resolving the problem. To begin with, if the chronically ill person realizes the possible effects of his illness on his self-image, he may be able to prevent himself from projecting these feelings on other people. The girl with the chronic blood disease felt she was a bother to her friends when they took her with them for a day's outing, but her friends didn't feel that way. A woman in a tubercular sanitarium felt her husband wouldn't want her anymore because she was sick, but her husband wanted her very much! It is, therefore, important for a person with an illness to realize this tendency to impose his or her feelings of low self-worth on other people. (These feelings may be only temporary.) If I don't like me, I will tend to feel that others don't like me and that perhaps even God doesn't like me. As one heroin addict said to me, "I can't reach out to God. I'm not good enough!" If I feel weak or inadequate, I will tend to believe that others see me as being weak. If a person succumbs to these fears and feelings of rejection, this may itself produce actual feelings of rejection because most people don't like to be tested constantly by an oversensitive person.

Not long ago I was recovering from a bout with the flu and didn't feel particularly well. Coming out of a grocery store, I ran into an acquaintance who has a lot of problems and is very touchy. I said hello, and she responded curtly in a tone of voice which clearly said, "Leave me alone." That I did. But later the woman called and said, "Why didn't you talk to me today?" In her usual way this woman was feeling inadequate, felt that I also thought she was inadequate, and proceeded to test me. Her abruptness was an attempt to see if I would go the second mile, so to speak, in making her feel accepted in spite of her rude behavior. Because I didn't feel well, I didn't let her push me; so her own feelings of self-rejection compelled me to reinforce that rejection.

Because a chronically ill person tends toward self-rejection, he or she must be particularly careful not to project those feelings onto others. He or she desperately needs the feelings of acceptance that come from good, close relationships.

Vital too is an attitude of acceptance of oneself when others really don't understand. And there will always be those around who have never been sick a day in their lives and feel that everyone should be equally healthy. These healthy individuals may feel that the ill person is a hypochondriac or a malingerer, even when objective evidence such as laboratory tests prove otherwise.

It is of even greater importance for the chronically ill to develop a new attitude toward the basis on which they evaluate their own sense of worth. The housewife who can't do all the physical work that a housewife normally performs may be of greater worth to her husband than the average woman because of her unique understanding and emotional support. She may have great talents in the arts or be a perceptive mother whose quality of time spent with her children is rare. Physical strength alone is certainly not the highest measure of a person's worth.

In an activist society it is important to realize that there is great worth in who a person is, not only in what he or she does.

Robert Browning said it well in his lines from "Rabbi Ben Ezra":

All I could never be,
All, men ignored in me,
This, I was worth to God, whose wheel the pitcher shaped.[1]

And again in "Bishop Blougram's Apology":

No, when the fight begins within himself,
A man's worth something. God stoops o'er his head,
Satan looks up between his feet—both tug—
He's left, himself, i' the middle: the soul wakes
And grows. Prolong that battle through his life!
Never leave growing till the life to come![2]

How a person handles pain, whether he or she turns it into self-pity or out toward understanding another person, is a measure of his or her worth. The Christian's attitude toward God and his acceptance of God's workings in his life are important measures of his worth. But such a relationship with God does not imply a weak sort of masochistic acceptance of pain. In speaking of handling emotional suffering, one woman wrote the following eloquent words to a friend: "The temptation so often is toward isolation and introspection, and yet I suppose this is the very thing we *dare* not give in to. The longer I live the more I begin to grasp that the choice in life is never between pain and no pain, or grief and no grief—it is rather a choice between *enduring* it and *using* it, and God, in his great patience, and with his own comfort, paves the way for its use. At least so I have found it again and again in my own experience." To use constructively the pain of a chronic illness should impart a great sense of worth to a person.

Not long ago a middle-aged man spoke to me of his frustration over a chronic, debilitating illness. He had been told by a number of presumably responsible people that his illness made him of less worth. In a pathetic, beaten-down way, he had accepted that viewpoint. Now he not only had to cope with the illness, medical expenses, and other pressures but he also felt belittled for being sick.

Actually a physical illness provides a platform for choice: it can make a person feel weak and inadequate, or it can provide ground for greater self-respect. "I, this person who hurts and feels weak, am still handling my life responsibly and feel greater compassion and empathy toward my fellow human beings than I was before capable of." When confronted with the need for choosing a viewpoint regarding illness and the possibility of a positive attitude, a person can go on with self-respect because suffering has meaning, a meaning over which he or she has some direct control.

At times other physical problems indirectly affect the emotions. A surgical procedure such as open heart surgery is one example. A cardiologist described to me the deep depression one man had developed after his surgery: "This man was not emotionally capable of handling open heart surgery. It should never have been done." Unfortunately the surgeon had not taken the man's emotions into consideration, and the trauma of the operation triggered some serious problems which might otherwise have remained dormant.

A middle-aged woman who was about to be married had

open heart surgery and afterwards, although the surgery was a success, claimed she felt terrible and decided not to get married. Only after some months had passed did she admit that she felt ugly because of the scar, too ugly to let a man look at her. A combination of psychological and medical treatment might have prevented the problem.

A physical disorder can produce psychological side effects. However, certain physical disorders have a direct biochemical result on the emotions. Traditional medicine has been aware of many of these for years. A low-functioning thyroid can cause either depression or anxiety while an overactive thyroid can cause anxiety. Indeed these psychological symptoms might well lead to a correct physical diagnosis. Addison's disease, a condition in which the adrenal glands are underactive, can cause anxiety. Hypoglycemia, discussed in a later chapter, has a myriad of psychological symptoms ranging from anxiety to depression.

Even anemia, a very common malady, has psychological effects. According to Dr. Granville F. Knight, a specialist in allergy and nutrition, anemic tissues do not get enough oxygen, and that factor can produce a depressive state as well as fatigue and weakness. He adds, "In anemia you often find that manganese, copper, and iron are all low, and the three work together in building up the hemoglobin."

Hormone levels are often a vital link to good mental health. According to Dr. Elrod premenstrual tension in a woman may be caused by a combination of fluid retention and an alteration of hormone levels. Furthermore, he feels that even though it is not completely understood postpartum psychosis (depression following childbirth) is partly hormonal; and the problems of menopause, while they are partly psychological and may vary from individual to individual, are also partly hormonal. As for the so-called male menopause, Dr. Elrod states that it is not as clear cut as female menopause; the age when it occurs is not as precise; and its existence is even questioned by many physicians. Yet he feels that the symptoms that seem connected with this phenomenon—skin irregularities, excessive sweating, easy fatigue, impotence, sleeplessness—cause psychological difficulties.

According to Dr. Knight, natural hormones given in the right amounts when needed may make a tremendous difference in how a woman feels. Depression, sweating, and lack of energy, when caused by a hormone imbalance, will be relieved almost completely by the use of estrogens. Dr. Knight also feels that the B complex vitamins are important in connection with the estrogens, particularly in the breakdown of excess amounts by the liver.

As to the male menopause, Dr. Knight feels that it does exist and that it may occur somewhere between the ages of forty and eighty but that the symptoms are less marked than in female menopause. He feels that the condition is partly hormonal and that testosterone has a good effect. Nevertheless, male menopause is also part of a psychological syndrome: Men become depressed because they feel they haven't lived enough and want one last fling.

Anyone who doubts the effect of the hormones on human emotions should look more closely at himself and at those around him. A preteenage girl habitually left her room in a messy state. Almost daily her parents reminded her to clean it up, with always the same answer from her, "I will, later." Then one day when her father came home from work, he walked by her open door. "Can't you clean this mess up?" he asked. His daughter burst into tears and threw herself on the bed. Confused, her father found his wife in the kitchen: "What's wrong with Nancy?"

"I'm afraid you're going to have to live with two females from now on," his wife answered.

Nancy had never been that sensitive, but then she had never been premenstrual before. Three weeks later she started her first period.

Such symptoms are not just true of adolescence although often they improve in adulthood. One middle-aged woman had great feelings of nervousness and anxiety before her periods each month. When in desperation she consulted her physician, he prescribed small amounts of hormones which almost immediately began to alleviate the symptoms.

In more recent years medical research has been involved in some areas which show an even greater potential for connecting certain physical disorders with behavioral problems. Much of this research falls outside the realm of traditional medicine, and understandably there is a great deal of controversy surrounding some of these opinions. Yet such doubt and controversy concerning new ideas has been true for the entire history of man. It is difficult to disregard the old, the known, for the unknown and sometimes untested. Only through a daring courage to change does man's knowledge progress.

Of great controversy has been the whole area of megavitamin treatment. Says Harvey M. Ross, M.D., a well-known orthomolecular psychiatrist in Los Angeles:

> Too many physicians have attempted to use megavitamins by giving inadequate doses of a few vitamins to the wrong people for an insufficient amount of time only to achieve the failure that could have been predicted. Unfortunately, they conclude that megavitamin therapy is a fraud rather than recognizing that they have not really followed the method as practiced by the orthomolecular psychiatrists. When this is done by an individual practitioner, it is sad enough, but when research physicians make the same error, it is inexcusable.[3]

Orthomolecular medicine is careful to state that where those factors missing in the body are replaced, "vitamins are only *part* of the treatment."[4] Yet the correct dosage of vitamins as part of a total treatment has been used, according to Dr. Ross, "with success in schizophrenia in adults and the childhood disorders of autism, schizophrenia, minimal brain dysfunction, learning disorders, and hyperactivity, in some neutrotic disorders, especially depression and anxiety, and in alcoholism and drug addiction."[5]

According to E. Cheraskin, M.D., and W. M. Ringsdorf, M.D., both from the University of Alabama, regarding vitamin needs, "Rarely does anyone fit the 'average requirement' mold, anyway."[6] On a group of so-called normal adults they found that, while 500 milligrams a day is supposed to be an adequate supply of tryptophane (the amino-acid precursor of niacin or vitamin B_3), the people tested still had emotional complaints when using even a 1000 milligrams as compared with those who were put on still higher doses. These physicians feel that the same principle is true for other nutritional elements.

If the average person does not fit the average requirement mold, then imagine what nutritional needs a person with symptoms and complaints may have. For example,

It has been demonstrated that some schizophrenics need huge amounts of Vitamin C. Studies have shown that normal people begin to excrete Vitamin C in their urine when given 4 grams a day. Among chronic schizophrenics who were tested, however, the dosage had to reach an average 40 grams a day before there was any spillover in the urine. The scientist who conducted that test learned, as a sidelight, that his group of schizophrenics got better when given these huge doses of ascorbic acid.[7]

According to Dr. Knight, high magnesium and calcium levels usually show up on a hair analysis test when that test is done on hypoglycemics. Comparing that result with samples done on urine specimens Dr. Knight feels that the condition indicates a rapid loss of calcium and magnesium, rather than too much taken in. In fact, says Knight, these people may actually feel *better* from calcium and magnesium supplements. His opinion has been affirmed by other researchers who agree that, as in the excessive need for vitamin C among some schizophrenics, there seems to be a greater need for magnesium and calcium among some hypoglycemics.

The behavioral aspects of all of these elements is more profound than has been previously recognized. A woman in her sixties was running a boarding house. Rather suddenly she seemed unable to keep efficient records, and she became forgetful to the point of needing someone else to look after things. Psychiatric help didn't alleviate the problem. In a final act of desperation she changed physicians and found one who correctly diagnosed her condition. Although she did not have dermatitis of the hands and neck, she had a brilliantly red tongue, a classic symptom of pellagra, a vitamin B deficiency state. She was put on large doses of vitamin B complex, orally and by injection, along with dessicated liver. Within six weeks she was running her own affairs again. Said the physician involved: "This is an extremely common condition in rest homes, and I think that a lot of people could get out of rest homes if they had enough of the right kind of vitamins."

The vitamin B complex which is composed of the various B vitamins appears to be a vital factor in good mental health. However, except for powdered yeast and dessicated liver or rice polishings, large dosages should be used only on the advice of a physician. According to Dr. Knight it is best not to use just one fraction of the B complex but rather to use the total B complex. When large doses of vitamin B_1 alone were given to rats, after two generations the males became sterile. While studies done with rats are not always comparable with those done on humans, they do give possible indications regarding human disorders.

Partly because the B complex is essential for enzyme function, a deficiency in humans can cause nervousness, anxiety, depression, fatigue, confusion, and difficulty in thinking and remembering, claims Dr. Knight.

Drs. Cheraskin and Ringsdorf quote Abram Hoffer, M.D., a pioneer in megavitamin therapy, as saying: "If *all* the vitamin B_3 were removed from our foods, everyone would become psychotic within one year."[8] Furthermore, "A *total* lack of vitamin B_3 leads to pellagra, but *low* levels produce humorless, overemotional, down-in-the-dumps individuals who are rarely recognized for what they are: 'minipellagrins.' "[9]

The use of B vitamins has been very effective in treating drug addicts. Dr. David Hawkins of the North Nassau Mental Health Clinic on Long Island feels that drug-oriented young people have been self-treating adverse drug reactions for a long time by the use of niacin (vitamin B_3) and honey, used to raise blood sugar levels. Says Dr. Hawkins: "As a group, members of the psychedelic drug culture reject most contemporary psychiatric approaches as being naive and lacking in basic awareness of basic principles that to them have already become everyday knowledge . . ."[10] Dr. Hoffer reportedly "uses massive doses of niacin to end a patient's prolonged LSD trip and to prevent the occurrence of undesirable side effects. He uses a dosage of 1 to 2 grams of niacin three times a day, plus tranquilizers if necessary."[11]

Again, Dr. Hawkins says that "the LSD Service for drug addicts has for years relied primarily on giving megavitamin doses and on attempting to raise blood sugar levels to counteract adverse psychedelic drug reactions."[12] He has found that high doses of vitamin B_1 (thiamine hydrochloride) can reduce the craving for Methedrine (speed). Dr. Ross uses several of the B vitamins, along with vitamins C and E, to treat heroin addiction.

Not yet mentioned, but of significant importance and central in the vitamins controversy, is vitamin E. According to Dr. Knight this vitamin is no longer "a vitamin looking for a disease." Dr. Knight feels that because vitamin E improves cellular oxidation, but slows the damage to cells caused by peroxidation of unsaturated fatty acids in cell walls, it is probably an anti-aging vitamin. It helps to prevent the toxic effect of smog on those who live in industrial areas. He offers as partial proof the fact that human cells grown in a culture live much longer if adequate vitamin E is added to the fluid. Yet, warns Dr. Knight, if a person has a valvular disease caused by rheumatic heart disease, then large doses of vitamin E can be dangerous, or even fatal. This is the only real contraindication. Medical supervision in the use of vitamins, in this case in even relatively small doses, is vital.

Minerals are also of significant importance to the emotional well-being of a person. According to Drs. Cheraskin and Ringsdorf, while zinc is only needed in small amounts, its deficiency is becoming more common due to changing food supplies and technology. Dr. Knight claims that children who are hyperactive sometimes show the presence of kryptopyrrholes in the urine which take out vitamin B_6 and zinc. The behavioral result is hyperactivity or depression. Very often these children have the characteristic white spots on their nails which indicate a zinc deficiency. Supplying them with zinc and vitamin B_6 changes their whole personality. Such a condition can be tested in one simple urine test; yet too often it goes unnoticed.

Magnesium is also very important since its deficiency causes a hyperirritability of the nervous system.

Dr. Willard Krehl of the University of Iowa, analyzing a group of patients with *mild* magnesium deficiencies, found that 22 percent had convulsions; 44 percent suffered hallucinations; 78 percent evidenced mental confusion; 83 percent were disoriented, couldn't remember where they were, the year, the day, the month; and 100 percent startled easily and were alarmed by unexpected movement or noise.[13]

Perhaps most vital of all to the nervous system is calcium. According to Dr. Knight a person who has a calcium deficiency will be jumpy and have difficulty in sleeping and in concentrating. A woman who is deficient in calcium may have frequent or severe menstrual cramps and cramps in the legs and muscles.

Drs. Cheraskin and Ringsdorf claim that "a tiny decrease of calcium in the blood can produce uncontrollable temper outbursts. The very young are extremely vulnerable. Babies have been known to hold their breath and turn blue; toddlers often have outrageous tempers." Furthermore, "Sudden, unexpected emotional stress or heavy physical exertion can raise lactate levels, thereby depleting circulating calcium in healthy people. You can protect yourself from the resulting nervous attacks by keeping your calcium reserves high. Extra calcium from cheese and other daily products is easily come by, and calcium supplements are readily available."[14] Adds Dr. Knight, "They should be balanced by extra magnesium."

Several patients of mine have been noticeably calmer and have completely solved sleep problems after their physicians began giving them calcium supplements. Calcium is not a cure for all anxiety and nervousness, but for many it seems to act as a powerful tranquillizer.

Other substances in the blood are relatively little known but yet significant to emotional health. Too little or too much serotonin can cause depression. Blood histamine levels, again if too high or too low, can make people nervous or depressed.

Not only do factors already present in the blood affect the emotions, but some which are introduced have a profound result. Lithium is a drug which, according to Dr. Knight, calms down the nervous system if given in a high enough concentration. This has been very helpful in the treatment of those suffering from manic-depression. It is a tricky drug to use, however, since its therapeutic dosage is just below the toxic level. Regular blood tests are essential for anyone taking lithium. Dr. Knight feels that a food allergy may also throw manic-depressives into either a manic or a depressive phase. His idea opens up a whole new area connecting physical with emotional problems— allergies.

In her book *Megavitamins*, Lynn Lilliston says:

> Other cases included a patient whose severe asthma was traced to corn: a child with behavior problems and failure to learn in school, due to allergens including beef and dust; a hyperactive boy allergic to numerous chemicals, and a woman with chronic fatigue and depression who reacted to mold. Another woman, whose deep depression had not responded to long-term psychiatric treatment, had been believed to be suffering a psychosomatic illness. It turned out she had an extreme reaction to peanuts.
>
> The biochemical reasons why some people display the symptoms of mental illness because of some food or element in their surroundings are not fully understood. Several different avenues of explanation are being explored. Still, doctors in the field are urging their colleagues to think of allergy when encountering the more puzzling cases of mental illness, those that do not fit in with easily recognized syndromes.[15]

Many allergy experts seem to agree that allergies can cause behavioral symptoms ranging from mild anxiety, fatigue, and depression to a so-called nervous breakdown and even a psychotic break.

Among a variety of techniques used to detect specific allergies, many doctors use a pulse test. The patient takes his pulse before eating a food, thirty minutes after, and then again in sixty minutes. If the pulse rises six to eight points above what it was before eating the food, an allergy is suggested. A generally rapid pulse may also be a good indicator of an allergy.

In such a discussion of the physical forces which may operate in an emotional problem, we wander into a never-never land. The surface is barely tapped. What we know from such a cursory glance as this is minimal. But even those asking the questions and doing involved research on one facet find more questions for every answer they receive. We come back to the ancient biblical statement: "You made all the delicate, inner parts of my body, and knit them together in my mother's womb. Thank you for making me so wonderfully complex! It is amazing to think about. Your workmanship is marvelous—and how well I know it" (Psa. 139:13, 14).

We have only the beginning of partial answers. But, debated as some of these views may be, they deserve a chance, proof that they are right or wrong and more money put into their research. It is important for a patient to be open to these new ideas if he or she is to succeed in the quest for health. Yet there must also be a healthy reserve, a questioning, a seeking of good medical opinion.

For most of us, the question arises: Is all that we are now finding out old information just now being discovered or are these disorders newly created? Most specialists I talked to agreed that both of those viewpoints were true. We are just now discovering some problems which have always plagued mankind, but our physical environment and our food supply have created some new problems.

We inhale smog and pesticides. We consume colors, pesticides, preservatives, and hundreds of other chemicals in our food. Reportedly, each of us now consumes five pounds of so-called certified synthetic colors a year. Our sugar intake is dangerously high. The result is an increase in viral infections, blood sugar irregularities, hyperactive children by the droves, and a general rundown state, physically and emotionally, in many people.

A small insight into this growing problem is revealed in a recent article in *Consumer Reports.* In a study of breakfast cereals, 70 percent of which is carbohydrate, much in the form of sugar. Rats fed with these high-sugar cereals grew only half as much as when they were fed the three highest rated cereals (those highest in protein and lowest in carbohydrates). "They also displayed at least one serious deficiency symptom, such as rickets, edema, tremors, emaciation, or dehydration (a poor diet can result in dehydration even when the rat gets plenty of water)."[16]

The report goes on to explain that while rats aren't humans they do eat the same kinds of foods as humans. They need just about the same nutrients except that they make their own vitamin C, and young rats need more protein in proportion to their body weight than do young children.

The children and many of the adults I see in my practice admit to the consumption of large amounts of cereals, soft drinks, candy, and desserts. The sugar content in these items is very high indeed, perhaps high enough to account for some nutritional deficiencies that didn't exist fifty years ago.

Added to the problems of modern-day nutrition is what Dr. Roger J. Williams calls the "metabolic profile." He says:

We need to develop techniques for identifying far more accurately than is now possible the inherited pattern of susceptibilities and resistances that is unique to each individual. Call it a 'metabolic profile' or any other name you wish, but plainly it represents a necessary precondition for making rational programs of nutrition tailored to fit each individual's special requirements. . . . we individually tend to be undernourished with respect to our special inherited requirements.[17]

Much debate has occurred regarding whether or not psychological problems are partially inherited. There are no clear-cut definitive answers in many cases. According to Dr. Knight, hereditary factors contribute to the incidence of hypoglycemia and allergies, both of which also produce behavioral problems in children and adults. It is interesting how often I will accurately suspect a metabolic disorder such as hypoglycemia in a person who turns out to have a family background of alcoholism (which is related to low blood sugar) or diabetes (which is connected to hypoglycemia in that it is an opposite type of blood sugar problem). In his writings psychiatrist Viktor Frankl refers to predisposing inherited factors in the person with an obsessive-compulsive personality.

One cannot with precision define and measure hereditary factors; but one only needs to walk through a hospital nursery of new-born infants to observe the inherited differences that exist apart from any environmental influences. Certainly among all those differences there are biochemical vulnerabilities as well as strengths.

At times in my work I am involved either in an adoption procedure or in counseling a small child who was adopted after infancy. My observations have reinforced the idea that a child's emotional state is not entirely due to his environment. One little boy was adopted at birth. His prenatal existence was a stormy period during which his natural mother was deciding whether or not to give him up for adoption. Yet when that child came home to his adoptive parents after two days in the hospital, he was one of the most calm, happy babies I have ever seen. From the first night, he slept straight through, and his physical and mental development has been very normal, even more advanced in some ways than the average child.

Thus among a number of reasons why I feel most parents should not feel excessive guilt over their children's problems is that a child's early environment may not be the primary cause of his disturbance. It seems possible that every human being is born with a different biochemical capacity for handling stress. Moreover, individuals may be born with varying vulnerabilities to different types of stress. For example, one child may react more severely than another to a death in the family. Obvious psychological factors help determine this behavior: the climate in the family for this child; how close he was to the deceased family member; how stable his early childhood was; his relationships with other members of the family; his friends, his school life; and how he views himself. Yet underlying all of these and other facets of the problem there may well be a hereditary biochemical predisposition which many psychologists have ignored for too long. Another child with an identical background and same set of circumstances but born with a different biochemical suit of clothes, may well have reacted differently. If such a biochemical factor exists, and I believe it does, then that becomes one of those subtle physical elements which effects adult emotional problems.

Finally, it is possible that the physical treatment of an infant at birth helps determine the state of his later emotional health. In an interview with Frederick LeBoyer, a French doctor, author, and filmmaker, Caterine Milinaire discovered his unique techniques in delivering children. Says LeBoyer, who prefers not to be labeled a doctor,

Each of us carries within, throughout life, the imprint of birth. As I was delivering those thousands of children I kept on wondering why those babies cried so much once they were born.

One day I started to get very interested in the newborn baby. This baby is born, cries, and often the more he cries the happier people are. They say, "The lungs are developing," or "This is a sign of strength," or some such inconsiderate conclusion. So I started looking at the newborn with a different eye. I thought this child should be content, feeling good, since at last he can move freely.[18]

LeBoyer interprets that first cry as a sound of "unlimited sadness." He attributes the baby's suffering to "the contrasts between what the infant has been through before and what he experiences at birth."[19] But the lack of understanding toward a child at birth as he experiences the fear of the unknown into which he has been plunged is also a factor. LeBoyer's main efforts have been aimed at easing this traumatic transition.

To protect the infant who has so far lived in darkness and muffled sound, LeBoyer delivers babies in a dimly lighted, silent room. The cord is not cut immediately in order to allow the baby two oxygen sources for a little while. The spine is handled carefully, and the baby is not roughly jerked upside down, for, says LeBoyer: "Whatever the treatment given to this little person at birth, the first contact outside the womb is bound to stay in a corner of his mind all of his life, and even though we cannot remember it, it becomes part of us." Furthermore, says LeBoyer, "Freud, W. Reich and Rank expressed it well in their work: distress stems from that first anxiety brought on by separation from the mother. It is manifest in two aspects: one physical, through oxygen deprivation when the cord is cut too soon and secondly by the emotional separation."[20]

Because the feeling of cloth on the skin is painful after having been in such a slippery environment, LeBoyer puts the child on the mother's abdomen where he can stretch by himself and feel the touch of his mother and father. Then, when the cord has stopped pulsating, it is cut.

At this point the baby is placed in a warm bath, with the water up to his neck. Then he opens his eyes and often smiles. The bath continues for three to six minutes. Then he is ready to be wrapped in cloth and to be still after living in constant movement for nine months. At times, later in infancy, this lack of movement may cause distress in a baby, which is why being held and rocked will help.

LeBoyer claims that babies born in this manner are happier and calmer. A woman whom I know had an experience in childbirth which to me helped confirm LeBoyer's point of view. After hearing of LeBoyer's ideas, Doris decided to have her baby by his method. At first her doctors fought the idea, claiming: "It's unnecessary; we turned out okay without it, didn't we?" Yet when she came to the end of her pregnancy still determined to have her baby by that method or change doctors, the physician involved gave in to her desire.

Although they did not put the baby on the mother's abdomen, they turned down the lights, minimized the voice levels, and waited to cut the cord. At birth the baby screamed as if in terror, which, by the way, is the kind of cry I have heard when I have witnessed a birth and is how a number of mothers have described their baby's first cry to me. The baby's cry stopped as he was placed into the water, as did the quivering of his lower lip. Afterwards he only whimpered, and since he has been home he has been very calm. The mother and father are delighted with the method and with their very easy-to-handle child.

LeBoyer's theories seem consistent with a new experimental treatment of premature babies. These infants are placed on water beds and exposed to the sound of a fetal heartbeat. The hope is that such treatment will protect the infants from crib death, a condition which is still somewhat of a mystery to the medical world. It seems obvious that buffering the transition from the womb to our world could well minimize the trauma of birth and thus produce calmer babies. If crib death has anything to do with the trauma of birth, then that too would certainly be prevented.

There has been a great emphasis in the past on the effect of the mind on the body, but we are now beginning to recognize that our outlooks and feelings are partly determined physically and metabolically. This new phase in medicine and psychotherapy is evolving slowly and at times grudgingly, for all of us resist change. Interestingly enough, Freud himself anticipated this possibility. He said:

> The future may teach us to exercise a direct influence, by means of particular chemical substances, upon the amounts of energy and their distribution in the apparatus of the mind. It may be that there are other undreamed-of possibilities of therapy. But for the moment we have nothing better at our disposal than the technique of psychoanalysis, and for that reason, in spite of its limitations, it is not to be despised.[21]

In later years Freud continued:

> I am firmly convinced that one day all these disturbances we are trying to understand will be treated by means of hormones or similar substances.[22]

A severely depressed young woman was hospitalized and fed the traditionally starchy food so common to psychiatric institutions and so detrimental to patients, many of whom are already suffering metabolic imbalances. A young doctor who had kept in touch with advances in orthomolecular medicine saw her and recognized the problem as being primarily metabolic. After proper diagnosis and appropriate treatment, mainly of her body, the depression lifted and she was released from the hospital. Today she functions well, and her depression remains only a bad dream.

Dr. Roger Williams makes a rather startling statement regarding mental illness:

> If you who read these words have never been afflicted with mental disease, it is not because you have undergone shock treatments or have consumed the right tranquilizers; it is because you have received in your food enough of all the minerals, amino acids, and vitamins that brain cells need to maintain them in reasonably good working order. It is possible that some other cells and tissues in your body have not fared as well, but that your brain, protected by nature as it is, has come through unscathed.
>
> If any one of a number of nutritional items had been received by your brain in, what would be for you, inadequate amounts, you would have been afflicted with mental disease.[23]

Dr. Williams is reputedly more responsible for original work in vitamin research than any living scientist. He concedes, however, that "It is well known that emotional states such as fear, hate, love, and stress cause biochemical changes to take place in the body, primarily through the operation of the endocrine glands." Furthermore, says Williams, "It is not at all impossible for brain biochemistry to be influenced by psychotherapy, nor is it impossible for biochemical changes to influence or help one's psyche."[24]

While not all emotional illness is primarily physical, some is; and in most cases a combination of physical, psychological, and spiritual factors are involved. A recognition of the influence of all three will give a better batting average to the psychiatric profession than has been true thus far.

NOTES

1. Donald Smalley, ed., *Poems of Robert Browning* (Boston: Mass.: (Riverside Press, 1956), p. 286.

2. Ibid., p. 205.

3. Harvey M. Ross, M.D., "Megavitamins," *Journal of Orthomolecular Psychiatry* 3, no. 4 (1974).

4. Ibid.

5. Ibid.

6. Dr. E. Cheraskin and Dr. W. M. Ringsdorf, Jr., with Arline Brecher, *Psychodietetics* (New York: Stein & Day, 1974), p. 93.

7. Lynn Lilliston, *Megavitamins: A New Key to Health* (Greenwich, Conn.: Fawcett Publications, Inc., 1975), p. 72.

8. Cheraskin and Ringsdorf, *Psychodietetics*, p. 92.

9. Ibid., p. 93.

10. Lilliston, *Megavitamins*, p. 170.

11. Ibid., p. 171.

12. Ruth Adams and Frank Murray, *Megavitamin Therapy* (New York: Larchmont Books, 1973), p. 186.

13. Cheraskin and Ringsdorf, *Psychodietetics*, p. 95.

14. Ibid., p. 92.

15. Lilliston, *Megavitamins*, p. 151.

16. "Which Cereals Are Most Nutritious?" *Consumer Reports*, February 1975, p. 77.

17. Dr. Roger J. Williams, *Nutrition against Disease* (New York: Bantam Books, Inc., 1973), p. 35.

18. Caterine Milinaire, "Born Happy," *Vogue*, July 1974, p. 81.

19. Ibid.

20. Ibid.

21. Sigmund Freud, *An Outline of Psychoanalysis*, (New York: W. W. Norton, 1949).

22. Sigmund Freud, quoted by Sackler, M. D., et al. in "Recent Advances in Psychobiology and Their Impact on General Practice," *Inter. Record of Med.* 170: 1551 (1957).

23. Williams, *Nutrition against Disease*, p. 155.

24. Ibid., p. 168.

CHAPTER 3

———— • ————

The New Problem
of Hypoglycemia

Charlene was a slight, tired-looking woman in her early twenties. She was referred to me for counseling because of frequent anxiety states which made her fearful of social situations, driving, going to the bank, and numerous other activities common to everyday living.

She had one small child who demanded more energy than she could give. Fortunately, her husband was patient and loved her enough to want her to get help.

After several sessions it became apparent to me that low blood sugar, or hypoglycemia, could be a part of her problem. She experienced frequent fatigue, particularly when she hadn't eaten. Often food quickly helped alleviate or even completely removed her symptoms. She had pain in the front of her head in the morning when she woke up. Certainly hypoglycemia seemed to be a possibility and should at least be ruled out.

When I questioned Charlene about that possibility, she quickly replied, "No, I don't have that. My doctor already told me I don't." Not liking to question his opinion, I still had my own conscience to live with; so I suggested that she try a physician who made more of a specialty of hypoglycemia. I gave her several names, and she chose a doctor near her home.

His diagnosis? Mild hypoglycemia, but severe enough to cause symptoms. The result? A great increase in the effectiveness of my counseling because it was combined with good medical treatment. A year later, she had almost no unpleasant symptoms and seemed very different from the woman who once said, "I no longer want to live if life is going to be this painful."

Because of the existing confusion over hypoglycemia there is danger either in ignoring its existence or in overdiagnosing and overtreating. Although it was written about over thirty years ago, in a sense it is a new disease because we have become aware of the problem on a wider scale and recognize some of its broader implications. As is the case with anything new, balance is important and should be guarded. The medical doctor who said to his colleague, "There is no such a thing as hypoglycemia," is ignoring a lot of medical and psychological evidence. However, those professionals who use the term *hypoglycemia* as a catchall for anything a patient complains about are as guilty of inaccuracy as those who slap a psychological label on everything they can't diagnose.

In a book which emphasizes the relationship of body, mind and spirit it has seemed important to place a special emphasis on hypoglycemia first of all because of the existing confusion just referred to. In my experience with patients, no single physical disorder has played as significant a role in my patients' psychological problems as that of hypoglycemia. I sometimes feel that it would indeed not be a bad idea if all people who seek psychological help would at some time early in their treatment be given a five-hour glucose tolerance test.

Hypoglycemia refers to a condition in which a person's blood sugar is abnormally low, as opposed to diabetes in which a person's blood sugar levels are excessively high. A five or six hour Glucose Tolerance Test is the usual and most reliable way of determining hypoglycemia. After either an overnight fast or a four-hour fast following a normal breakfast, a sample of blood is taken, and the patient is given a glucose drink, usually containing 100 grams of sugar. Blood is then drawn periodically over a five- or six-hour period.

According to E. M. Abrahamson, M.D., in *Body, Mind, Sugar*, in the normal patient, "the initial blood sugar level should lie between 80 and 120 mg per 100 cc of blood. The level should rise to not more than 160 in thirty or sixty minutes, and it should return to its initial value within two hours."[1]

In the person with hypoglycemia the blood sugar levels drop

lower than normal in a pattern that varies from one individual to another. At what point a sugar level becomes abnormal has been a matter of great debate among physicians. Furthermore, it is not only how low the sugar level drops that is significant, but how fast that drop occurs and how great the difference is between the highest and lowest level.

Some doctors recognize hypoglycemia only when there is a very low, precipitous drop in the sugar, such as that caused by a pancreatic tumor which is, by the way, quite rare. Others are increasingly recognizing that functional hypoglycemia, a malfunctioning within the body usually involving the production of insulin rather than organic disease, is a demonstrable medical problem even if the blood sugar levels are not extremely low.

Dr. Harvey Ross defines hypoglycemia clearly when he says:

> If the fasting level is very low, for example, below 60 milligrams percent, or, if one of the blood samples falls to around 30 milligrams percent, the physician should be suspicious that this hypoglycemia may be caused by a physical reason as mentioned before, and further tests may be ordered. The following discussion concerns the cases with no known cause.
>
> After the test is done, it must be interpreted correctly. If one of the specimens falls below 50 milligrams percent, a diagnosis of reactive hypoglycemia is made. Of the no-known-cause group, the reactive hypoglycemics represent only about 5 percent of the cases I see. A far more prevalent group of hypoglycemia is the group known as relative hypoglycemia, described by Salzer. This embodies Roger Williams' important concept of individuality. One person may get along very well with a blood sugar of 70 milligrams percent, whereas another person may need 90 milligrams percent to have a normally functioning brain. How then can the criteria for diagnosis be so statically defined as having to fall below 50 milligrams percent before a diagnosis is made? In the relative hypoglycemic group, if the blood sugar on any of the specimens is more than 20 milligrams percent below the fasting level, or falls more than 50 milligrams percent in one hour, and these changes are accompanied by symptoms of hypoglycemia, the diagnosis of relative hypoglycemia is made. The proof that

this is a valid concept is in the improvement obtained in a large number of cases. Other abnormal curves qualifying as hypoglycemia are the flat curve, which is the failure of the blood sugar to rise 50 percent above the fasting specimen during the first hour, and the saw tooth curve, which is a marked rise of the blood sugar after the return to the fasting specimen level at the second hour.[2]

As far back as 1942 Dr. Sidney Portis of the College of Medicine of the University of Illinois made a preliminary report on his work in blood sugar to the American Psychosomatic Society. From his work between the years 1944 and 1950 Dr. Portis concluded, as reported by Abrahamson, that even in patients who exhibit a "flat curve" on the Glucose Tolerance Test, where the blood sugar levels do not rise very high nor drop very low at any point in the test, there are significant symptoms of fatigue, shakiness, vertigo, sweating, and at times, anxiety. Hypoglycemia, according to Abrahamson, is also characterized by crying spells, nervousness, hunger, and confusion.

Because of the perplexing array of symptoms as well as medical disagreement, hypoglycemia can be very difficult to diagnose. However, if a person shows a low reading on the Glucose Tolerance Test, experiences some hypoglycemic symptoms during the test, and in general presents these symptoms during his everyday life, hypoglycemia would seem to be a fairly obvious conclusion.

The chart showing the various levels on the six-hour Glucose Tolerance Test and one opinion of interpretation of those levels may provide a guideline.

For comparison, actual cases involving the shorter test have been included to demonstrate diabetic curves. The small figures above the segments of each curve indicate the amounts of glucose (in grams) excreted during that period. The different curves are:

1. An exceedingly mild case of diabetes. Notice that the fasting blood glucose level is quite normal. The patient was, for all practical purposes, only potentially diabetic. He need only avoid excessive amounts of sweets.

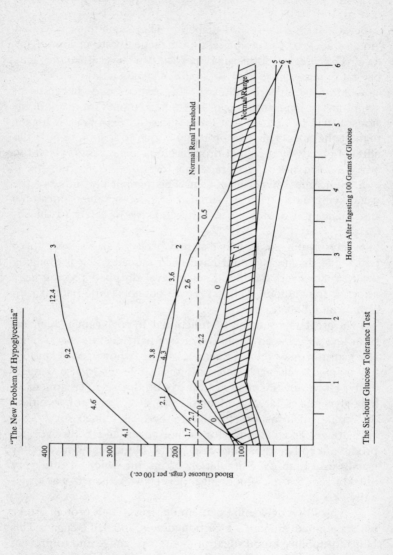

"The New Problem of Hypoglycemia"

The Six-hour Glucose Tolerance Test

2. A moderately severe case of diabetes. This patient must take insulin.

3. An extremely severe diabetic. This sometimes is called "total diabetes," for the patient has practically no insulin of his own. The rise in blood sugar persists for several hours. This patient requires more than 100 units of insulin a day.

4. Manifest hyperinsulinism. This patient had the classical symptoms of hyperinsulinism. She "blacked out" on many occasions. It will be noticed that the level at the sixth hour is higher than at the fifth. This rise probably is due to stimulation of the adrenal glands by the great drop in blood sugar, after which the adrenal hormones begin to raise that level.

5. Subclinical hyperinsulinism. This patient had none of the usual symptoms of hyperinsulinism. She complained only of a state of mental depression which yielded completely to the dietary treatment.

6. Dysinsulinism. If this test had been made for only three hours, the diagnosis would have been diabetes. On prolonging the test, however, the blood sugar level dropped precipitously after the fourth hour. This curve was obtained on a patient with asthma and diabetes.[3]

In a great many cases of functional hypoglycemia, high insulin levels produced by an overactive pancreas are also found. High insulin may reduce sugar levels in hypoglycemia, just as low insulin levels in diabetes allow sugar levels to rise dangerously. However, this may not always be the case. Treatment of hypoglycemia is largely oriented toward diet control, avoiding or limiting such insulin stimulating foods as refined sugar, carbohydrates, and caffeine; for, while sugar and carbohydrates produce a rather rapid increase in the blood sugar level, they usually cause an overstimulation of insulin which in turn very quickly reduces the blood sugar level lower than it was originally.

A typical hypoglycemia diet emphasizes a high protein intake with a limited amount of carbohydrates and fruit sugar. This helps to stabilize blood sugar in the normal range and to prevent sudden drops. Frequent small meals are important since blood sugar levels can sometimes fall to symptomatic levels in from one to three hours after eating. Some supportive medical treatment along with vitamin and mineral supplements is also used by many doctors. In most cases of functional hypoglycemia other glands, such as the thyroid and adrenal, may be involved. In many cases the liver, which regulates the release of glucose into the blood, may be affected. Thus treatment is very individualized, depending on which glands are malfunctioning.

In general, for a great many hypoglycemics, the following diet, modified slightly from that of Dr. Seale Harris, may be helpful.

DIET FOR HYPERINSULINISM

On Arising—Medium orange, half grapefruit, or 4 ounces of juice.
Breakfast—Fruit or 4 ounces of juice; 1 egg with or without two slices of ham or bacon; ONLY ONE slice of any bread or toast with plenty of butter; beverage.
2 Hours after Breakfast—4 ounces of juice.
Lunch—Meat, fish, cheese, or eggs; salad (large serving of lettuce, tomato, or Waldorf salad with mayonnaise or French dressing); vegetables if desired; ONLY ONE slice of any bread or toast with plenty of butter; dessert; beverage.
3 Hours after Lunch—8 ounces of milk.
1 Hour before Dinner—4 ounces of juice.
Dinner—Soup if desired (not thickened with flour); vegetables; liberal portion of meat, fish, or poultry; ONLY ONE slice of bread if desired; dessert; beverage.
2–3 Hours after Dinner—8 ounces of milk.
Every 2 Hours until Bedtime—4 ounces of milk or a small handful of nuts.

Allowable Vegetables—Asparagus, avocado, beets, broccoli, Brussels sprouts, cabbage, cauliflower, carrots, celery, corn, cucumbers, eggplant, Lima beans, onions, peas, radishes, sauerkraut, squash, string beans, tomatoes, turnips.

Allowable Fruits—Apples, apricots, berries, grapefruit, melons, oranges, peaches, pears, pineapple, tangerines.

May be cooked or raw, with or without cream but without sugar. Canned fruits should be packed in water, not syrup.

Lettuce, mushrooms, and nuts may be taken as freely as desired.

Juice—Any unsweetened fruit or vegetable juice, except grape juice or prune juice.

Beverages—Weak tea (tea ball, not brewed); decaffeinated coffee; coffee substitutes. May be sweetened with saccharin.

Desserts—Fruit, unsweetened gelatin, junket (made from tablet, not mix).

Alcoholic and Soft Drinks—Club soda, dry ginger ale, whiskies, and other distilled liquors.

AVOID ABSOLUTELY—Sugar, candy, and other sweets, such as cake, pie, pastries, sweet custards, puddings, and ice cream.

Caffeine—ordinary coffee, strong brewed tea, beverages containing caffeine. (Your doctor will tell you what these are.)

Potatoes, rice, grapes, raisins, plums, figs, dates, and bananas.

Spaghetti, macaroni, and noodles.

Wines, cordials, cocktails, and beer.[4]

According to Abrahamson this diet should be followed for about three months. Then a tapering-off diet such as the following can be used:

MODIFIED HYPERINSULINISM DIET
FOR TAPERING-OFF

Breakfast—Fruit or juice; cereal (dry or cooked) with milk or cream and/or 1 egg with or without two slices of ham or bacon; only one slice of bread or toast with plenty of butter; beverage.

Lunch—Meat, fish, cheese or eggs; salad (large serving of lettuce, tomato, or Waldorf salad with mayonnaise or French dressing); buttered vegetables if desired; only one slice of bread or toast with plenty of butter; dessert; beverage.

Midafternoon—Glass of milk.

Dinner—Soup if desired (not thickened with flour); liberal portion of meat, fish, or poultry; vegetables; potatoes, rice, noodles, spaghetti, and macaroni (may be eaten in moderation only with this meal); one slice of bread if desired; dessert or crackers and cheese; beverage.

Bedtime—Snack (milk, crackers and cheese, sandwich, fruit, etc.).

All vegetables and fruits are permissible. Fruit may be cooked or raw, with or without cream but without sugar. Canned fruits should be packed without sugar.

Lettuce, mushrooms, and nuts may be taken as freely as desired.

Juice—Any unsweetened fruit or vegetable juice except grape juice or prune juice.

Beverages—Weak tea (tea ball, not brewed); decaffeinated coffee; coffee substitutes. May be sweetened with saccharin.

Desserts—Fruit; unsweetened gelatin; junket (made from tablets, not from mix).

Alcoholic and soft drinks—Club soda, dry ginger ale, whiskies, and other distilled liquors.

AVOID ABSOLUTELY—Sugar, candy, and other sweets, cake, pie, pastries, sweet custards, puddings, and ice cream. Caffeine—ordinary coffee, strong brewed tea, and other beverages containing caffeine.

Wines, cordials, cocktails, and beer.[5]

At the end of the diet period some patients may be able to maintain as long as they avoid most sweets and caffeine and *always* eat a bedtime snack.

At this point great emphasis should be made on the need for a patient to consult a physician who is knowledgeable in this area. For example, while the above diet is important and fits many people's needs, it may not fit yours. Don't self-diagnose and self-prescribe. Yet, on the other hand, no physician or psychotherapist is God. If you doubt a professional opinion on this particularly debatable disorder, consult someone else. Most physicians will accept your desire for a consultation. If they don't, it's your body that's at stake, so seek another opinion anyway.

This disorder is sometimes difficult to detect because of its varied symptoms. One girl who had been diagnosed as an epileptic turned up with an extremely low curve on the Glucose Tolerance Test—low enough to account for epilepticlike seizures. An alcoholic made a complete recovery, partially by a change in diet and the addition of vitamin supplements.

Even normal people can at times have hypoglycemiclike symptoms. A house guest of mine ate a large quantity of sugary food and within an hour evidenced shakiness and weakness. After she drank a glass of orange juice, her symptoms disappeared, and she didn't know what had happened. She had been overly tired. That plus the sugar caused an overproduction of insulin which in turn reduced her sugar level. For a few moments she felt some hypoglycemic symptoms; yet there is every evidence that she is not truly a hypoglycemic.

Some physicians report that they are finding many children who present hypoglycemic symptoms which disappear after a proper diet is introduced. Many of these children fit into the hyperactive category. When I have noticed these indications in my patients, it has been largely through the symptom of craving sugar. One little girl repeatedly added five sugar cubes to each cup of already-sweetened hot chocolate. Another liked to eat the sugar cubes alone! Both were having behavioral problems and tired easily. The problem of childhood hypoglycemia should not be overlooked; it may, in my opinion, contribute greatly to a child's emotional difficulties.

From a psychological point of view there are some important

implications in hypoglycemia since some of the symptoms are anxiety, confusion, and in some cases depression. This combination of psychological and physical factors is true of many diseases, but hypoglycemia is particularly prone to this combination because it is a metabolic disorder related to glandular functioning and diet. After speaking of the effect of diet on emotions, W. D. Currier, M.D., states in his article "Nutritional Aspects of Stress," published in the *Journal of Applied Nutrition*:

> Malnutrition thus produces emotional stress and strain. But the reverse is just as true. The various nutritional elements are burned up in prodigious amounts under conditions of emotional tension.[6]

Sometimes hypoglycemia alone produces psychological symptoms. For example, during a sugar drop a person may suddenly feel apprehensive for no apparent reason. At other times the drop in sugar may precipitate or amplify an existing problem. This would be true of the person who fears examinations in college but finds them intolerable during a sugar drop or of the already angry businessman who keeps a leash on his anger until the sugar drop makes that anger harder to control.

As one physician told me, if a normal person were suddenly injected with insulin, the resulting drop in sugar would very quickly produce feelings of fear.

Such a view seems consistent with that of Dr. Harvey Ross who found that when hypoglycemia is treated medically usually one of two things happen psychologically. Some patients have the same problems, like difficulty at home, but can handle them better. Now they can cope. Others feel better physically but still have problems which they want to work out in psychotherapy. Says Dr. Ross, "Once the medical problems are dealt with, psychotherapy is more effective and the person now has the energy to work on his problems."

Whether hypoglycemia acts as a causative agent or as a precipitating force, just living with hypoglycemic symptoms for any length of time creates a unique set of psychological problems. Chronic fatigue alone lowers one's sense of good self-esteem. Such lowered self-worth is only made worse if a physician tells you that there is no medical reason for your symptoms and if psychotherapy does not prove to be a complete answer because of the underlying medical problem which has not been treated.

The possible result of such a dilemma was exhibited by the forty-five-year-old patient I saw who said her doctor had told her that her blood sugar levels were abnormal but had sent her to get psychological help without supportive medical treatment. She ended up with three or four different psychotherapists who ignored the importance of her physical problem and who, indeed, told her that her problem was entirely psychological. She was told to ignore her fatigue and dizziness, which was impossible for her to do. Her very inability to do as they said made her feel just that much more inadequate. By the time she got to me, she gave up before she started. She felt that she was beyond help and that she had to live out her life with fatigue, dizziness, and depression. Nothing could induce her to get further medical or psychological help. Having tried for so long, she couldn't face the possibility of another failure. She now sits home feeling completely defeated. She finds little joy in life and cannot stand the possible disappointment of ever going to another physician, much less starting another round of psychotherapy.

In the patients I have seen who receive correct medical treatment, counseling becomes in general much easier and more effective. One patient told me that she wanted to die or be committed to an institution where she could feel safe. Another described her fear of supermarkets, unless the market was relatively empty. Another sat in my office and literally shook as she tried to hold a cup of coffee. Another wanted to quit work because of his fear. All of these people got over the symptoms with a combination of weekly counseling sessions and medical treatment for hypoglycemia. Their blood sugar levels on a Glucose Tolerance Test ranged from a low of 43 to the "flat curve" type test result previously mentioned. It is, of course, impossible to tell exactly where the medical treatment helped and where the counseling did.

A middle-aged woman who was afraid when confronted with social situations made fairly good progress before she was diagnosed as having hypoglycemia. She had started visiting more with friends and had even invited a couple of people over for dinner. After her treatment for hypoglycemia began, however, the progress in counseling was much greater and quicker. Her shakiness stopped almost immediately, which helped her feel more at ease when she served food. She was less tired, more confident, more easily convinced to try to do more. Counseling helped in spite of the hypoglycemia. And, presumably, medical treatment would have helped without counseling. But ideally the two seemed to work more satisfactorily together.

However, there are some inherent pitfalls in the psychological treatment of the hypoglycemic. As is true in any physical disease, but perhaps more so in hypoglycemia because of the psychological overlay, some people use the problem as a copout. One patient announced he was not going to work anymore because "I'm sick; I have hypoglycemia." Another dropped out of counseling for a while, although he came back, because he "had chemical factors determining his behavior and therefore it was all physical." In actuality this man had obvious psychological problems from way back which hypoglycemia had only amplified and made worse.

Such destructive attitudes are unwittingly fostered by the remarks of physicians who go overboard in their attempt at bedside manner and say things such as, "Your sugar is so low I don't know how you've made it this far." Or "How do you get up in the morning?" Or "Most people with your problem wouldn't even be able to work." These statements are meant to be sympathetic to a patient who has often been told he is lazy or not sick at all or he's just got psychological hang-ups. But they can go too far and often become crippling.

A young man recently sat in my office and said: "I have just found out that I have hypoglycemia, and I have to go back for more tests. My doctor says I'm in terrible shape, and I'm really tired of trying. I think I'll just quit for a while." The doctor who sounded as if he meant well had no idea of the negative effect he had on his patient.

A better approach is to admit that the person does have a physical problem, with or without some psychological overlay, but to encourage the patient to live as free from self-pity and self-preoccupation as possible.

This is accomplished partly by the attitude which the medical doctor and/or psychotherapist projects. His optimism and belief in the patient's ability to become well, and his estimate of the patient's worth while he regains his health, will greatly influence the patient's attitude.

Furthermore when a patient is diagnosed as hypoglycemic, every effort should be made to give him or her a balanced view of the problem. The patient should be informed that the disorder is treatable; that he or she will almost always feel better if proper treatment is maintained; and that hypoglycemia is not entirely psychological but some psychological help may be warranted. Above all, the hypoglycemic needs understanding, not pity.

Sometimes even the treatment of hypoglycemia helps the patient develop a hypochondriacal pattern. Some hypoglycemic diets measure out with great precision each meal and snack during the day. Between eating frequently throughout the day, weighing food, cooking from a hypoglycemia cookbook, taking all kinds of vitamin supplements, reading the mass of material on the subject which has been printed, and in general watching one's body constantly for a sugar drop, anyone could quickly become introverted and self-occupied. While some of the above practices are necessary to a degree, some patients in going to extremes become invalids of their own making and become unwilling to face problems and solve them.

According to Dr. Granville Knight, such precision with food is not generally necessary. Regarding food intake in general, Dr. Knight says in his booklet "Physical Degeneration and the Allergic Diathesis," "Avoid sugar and bleached flours . . . concentrate on a diet of milk, meat, fowl, fish, animal organs, such as liver, brain, tripe, sweetbreads and kidneys, whole grain bread, green and yellow vegetables, potatoes (broiled or baked), salads and fruit."[7] Dr. Knight's treatment of hypoglycemia is of course more specific than this one short quotation, but he wisely avoids treating hgypoglycemia as a medical or diet fad.

To have hypoglycemia is to have a condition which requires medical treatment and diet control. At times it may produce or amplify problems which require psychological treatment. Just as psychological treatment without medical attention may not sufficiently help the patient, so medical treatment without psychological aid, when that is required, may be less than effectual. Whatever the treatment, the patient's attitude toward his problem is of primary importance.

Viktor Frankl in his book, *The Doctor and the Soul*, speaks of the uniqueness of every man's existence in all conditions of life. He says, "Life requires of man spiritual elasticity, so that he may temper his efforts to the chances that are offered."[8] Regarding what he calls "limiting factors upon his life," Frankl says, "His [man's] very response to the restraints upon his potentialities provides him with a new realm of values which surely belong among the highest values."[9]

With any medical or psychological problem a patient has two choices: get all the treatment which is appropriate and learn to live with any residuals that remain, or cease trying and dissolve in self-pity. Such residuals may be physical, such as a tendency toward fatigue. Certainly most hypoglycemics will live indefinitely on a restricted diet. Even the tendency to some apprehension or depression may continue, but if the patient is careful and does not push himself or herself, usually the residuals will be minimal. It is the responsibility of every person in the various helping professions to encourage the hypoglycemic away from absorption in his or her problem and toward a life in which he or she may feel fulfilled and useful.

Hypoglycemia is being written about extensively and discussed wherever people come together, whether it be a TV talk show or a private dinner party. The scope of the conversation often goes far beyond that of a disorder causing fatigue. Many articles I have read and physicians I have talked to indicate a correlation between hypoglycemia and problems such as smoking and alcoholism. Dr. Harvey Ross and others feel that there is a definite relationship between schizophrenia and hypoglycemia. Many schizophrenics have hypoglycemia, but most hypoglycemics do not become schizophrenics. In the same fashion many alcoholics have hypoglycemia while most hypoglycemics are not alcoholics. During the last five years I have worked with several hundred adolescent drug users. Many of these young people find that eating foods high in sugar content helps bring them down more rapidly from an LSD trip. Furthermore almost all marijuana smokers describe a time of intense desire for food following smoking the marijuana. They describe this as the "Marijuana Munchies."

It was of interest to me to talk to Dr. Hardin B. Jones who has interviewed over sixteen hundred drug users. He too reports that some LSD users claim that eating sugar helps to come down from an LSD trip. Dr. Jones feels that after smoking marijuana there is probably a slight increase in blood sugar, followed in two or three hours by a hypoglycemic condition.

It would seem that in hypoglycemia we have a far-reaching, complicated problem which has a way of presenting questions at a faster rate than answers.

William Greenway of Harbor General Hospital in Los Angeles, California, states that the "disease definitely exists." The problem according to him is to know what complaints in any one given case are accounted for by hypoglycemia. He, and many others, agree that there are extremes at both ends of the spectrum. As such, hypoglycemia can still be easily ignored or perhaps made to account for some symptoms which are mainly psychological or arise from some other source.

William Cole, in his article "Hypoglycemia—Shortage of Body Fuel," *Today's Health*, argues that hypoglycemia has become a catchall for anything that ails a person and wisely warns against allowing the questions that remain unanswered to prevent treating the many who are being and could be benefitted from such treatment. Retorts Cole:

> Certainly it *could* be something else. What if it does give some hypochondriacs another imagined ailment? Does that mean it

should be ignored? Fortunately for those who are affected, who are chugging along short of body fuel, hypoglycemia, after lurking for decades in the shadow of diabetes, is finally coming into the light.[10]

NOTES

1. E. M. Abrahamson, M.D., and A. W. Pezet, *Body, Mind, and Sugar* (New York: Holt, Rinehart, & Winston, 1951), p. 38.

2. Harvey M. Ross, M.D., Hypoglycemia," *Journal of Orthomolecular Psychiatry* 3: 242 (1974).

3. Abrahamson and Pezet, *Body, Mind, and Sugar*, p. 55.

4. Ibid., pp. 68–69.

5. Ibid., pp. 105–6.

6. W. D. Currier, M.D., "Nutritional Aspects of Stress," *Journal of Applied Nutrition* 10, no. 3 (1957).

7. Granville Knight, M.D., "Physical Degeneration and the Allergic Diathesis," *The Transactions* (American Society of Ophthalmologic and Otolaryngologic Allergy, 1968) 9, no. 1.

8. Viktor E. Frankl, *The Doctor and the Soul* (New York: Bantam, 1967), p. 34.

9. Ibid., p. 35.

10. William Cole, "Hypoglycemia—Shortage of Body Fuel," *Today's Health*, November 1968.

CHAPTER 4

---•---

You Are What You Think

"You have pretty eyebrows," said a seven-year-old boy, looking up at the waitress who had just brought coffee to his mother and me.

The waitress sputtered out a confused, "Thank you," and walked quickly to another table. Yet her movements from then on were interesting to watch. From a woman who looked tired, moved slowly and had been rather curt in answer to questions regarding the menu, she became almost cheerful and certainly looked more energetic.

Who has not known the feeling of renewed energy from a kind word or a friendly smile? Conversely, most of us have experienced the destructive effects of the mind on the body: the tight muscles and dry mouth right before a public appearance or an examination; the fast heartbeat and accelerated muscular movements right before an automobile accident; and the numb feeling of shock that occurs after the pronouncement of a tragic message such as the death of a loved one or a bad medical prognosis. Like it or not, our bodies are constantly affected by our minds for both good and bad.

In my work I see the mind-body relationship a little more dramatically perhaps than the average person. A young teenager was on heavy dosages of a rather dangerous medication because of a rash which resisted medical treatment. After a number of physicians had failed to find a medical cause for the rash, she was sent to me at their request as a kind of last attempt. The first significant insight I had into her problem was that when she was happy the rash subsided; but when she had to do something she disliked, such as take a piano lesson, she immediately developed a rash. And it worked. Once she had a good rash going, her whole family gave in to her—she didn't take the lesson, or go to school, or visit her parent's friends. I suspect that not even Jenny realized how much of a weapon that rash was.

Through counseling which included both her and her parents, Jenny learned some positive ways to meet her needs, and her family learned not to be intimidated by the rash. The rash completely disappeared, and there was no further need for medication. Actually, the medication was discontinued before the rash was gone because both her physician and I were convinced that it was basically ineffective in her case.

Rashes are only one possible manifestation of psychological distress. A little girl of eight had constant colds and had missed more days of school than she had attended. When her parents brought her for counseling for an entirely different reason, her colds began to disappear along with other symptoms. Now, a year after counseling was discontinued, she is the healthiest person in her family and is very proud of that fact.

A middle-aged man came to talk about his son's drug problem but soon divulged the fact that often after he and his son fought he felt almost paralyzed in his legs and arms. When the son would leave the house for a few days, the father's arms and legs would feel normal again.

A ten-year-old boy happily told me about his week at camp. Then suddenly as he talked about his mother and coming home, his speech trailed off and he began to get very frightened. "I'm seeing double," he cried. "Something's wrong with my eyes." As I calmed him by talking about camp again, he dropped his eye complaints and was seeing quite normally when he left my office. We checked with an ophthalmologist later to be sure there was no physical problem involved. His opinion concurred with mine: The eyes had simply responded to the negative stress relating to the boy's feelings about his mother.

I am not implying that all rashes, colds, or other physical problems are always psychosomatic or psychogenic, but some are, and others are both physically and psychologically induced. Many times psychological stress merely brings out a physical vulnerability. For example, a person who has a hereditary predisposition to diabetes may develop diabetes under extreme emotional stress. A person without that predisposition might never become diabetic. On the other hand, a person with a tendency toward diabetes might never have a diabetic problem if his life is relatively free from undue stress.

The physiological aspects of the effect of the mind on the body are complicated and not altogether understood. Hardin B. Jones, Ph.D., professor of physiology and medical physics at the University of California at Berkeley, claims that under extreme stress, such as anger or fear, there are changes in brain function which account for a symptom similar to sleeplessness. Sympathetic nervous system activity increases as does adrenal production. These changes become cyclical, self-perpetuating themselves and causing other changes.

Dr. Calvin Elrod describes other changes that occur in the body as a result of emotional stress. He says the body prepares itself for some kind of protective activity such as physical defense or escape. The blood vessels tighten or constrict, sending the blood pressure up and providing the brain with more blood. Since the body needs energy, glycogen is released from the liver, and the greater need for oxygen may produce hyperventilation or rapid breathing. The sweat glands oversecrete, and the salivary glands slow down causing dryness of the mouth. The intestinal tract empties as does the bladder.

When all of these bodily reactions occur, there is a need for a corresponding outlet. Unless there is a contraindication such as heart disease, the best immediate reaction is physical activity such as running around the block or a quick swim.

There are, however, according to Dr. Elrod, some people who experience these kinds of severe stress reactions daily, indeed almost momentarily. To such people a rejection by a business colleague may bring on as severe a set of reactions as impending physical danger or even death. Thus the body is in a constant stress situation, and such people tend to develop sleeplessness, high blood pressure, overacidity, nervousness, perspiration, or far more complicated physical problems.

It is imperative to emphasize the *reality* of physical disorders which arise from stress. A heart attack, which may follow years of prolonged stress and mismanagement of that stress both physically and psychologically, is terribly real as is the death that may occur from such an attack. I have seen people with blinding headaches or severe stomach cramps told, "Snap out of that. It's just nerves." It may be "just nerves," but it still hurts. Somehow many people illogically think that if the emotions cause a physical problem the pain can be turned off with an act of will much as one turns off a light with the flip of a switch. In actuality this lack of understanding of psychosomatic problems only adds to a person's stress and compounds the physical ailment.

Stress in itself is neither bad nor escapable. It is part of all life and can motivate great deeds. But stress becomes destructive in excessive amounts or when a person's reactions to it are extreme. For example, a housewife who has outside interests will probably be more psychologically healthy than the woman who is confined exclusively to home and family. But if she tries to raise four children, please her husband, hold down a full-time job, and fulfill a large number of social commitments, the stress is likely to be too great. Or, if this same woman keeps her commitments down to a comfortable level but is excessively threatened by people's criticisms, the stress can also be too great.

Dr. Hans Selye, a Canadian doctor whose name is more connected with stress than any other living being, says:

> Stress is the wear and tear of everyday life; it's a part of everything we do. We can't avoid it, nor would we want to, because the absence of stress is death. The idea is not to try to avoid stress, but to make sure we live with beneficial stress—that is, feelings of pleasure, fulfillment, satisfaction. If we feel worthy and loved, we are less likely to develop the diseases that we now know are related to harmful stress or *distress*.[1]

A constructive handling of stress is largely dependent upon a person's self-image. A good sense of personal worth is partially dependent on the ability generally to avoid overcommitment. To be healthfully selfish and say no means in the long run to preserve oneself so that an optimum of valuable life-tasks can be performed. If I take on more patients than I can handle, I will probably not do as well as I should with any of them, which in turn is not good for my self-image. If the housewife overcommits herself, nothing will be done well, which in turn will only feed her feelings of inadequacy.

Likewise, the housewife's stress which arises from the criticisms of others effects her self-image. People who like themselves, in the correct sense of that word *like*, will not be crushed by unfair criticism and will grow from criticism which is warranted—although they still won't enjoy it, for no one cares to have his or her weaknesses exposed.

In spite of the great importance of a healthy self-image, it is often overlooked or not even understood, particularly within some religious circles.

Self-esteem is the evaluation one makes of his or her worth. It is possible to overestimate or underestimate that worth. Biblical principles along this line are consistent with sound psychology. Kenneth Wuest translates Romans 12:3, "For I am saying through the grace which is given to everyone who is among you, not to be thinking more highly of one's self, beyond that which one ought necessarily to be thinking, but to be thinking with a view to a sensible appraisal (of oneself) according as to each one God divided a measure of faith."

To be able honestly to appraise oneself is a wonderful experience, for then a person can feel good about who he or she is and yet be free to change what he or she doesn't like. One of the rewarding aspects of counseling is to see people begin to *feel* that they're really okay. They articulate this in different ways, of course. One nurse said, "I can walk into the lab now without that horrible self-conscious feeling that everyone is looking at me." A businessman said, "I know I'm good at my job now, so I don't worry so much about losing it." A child whose elevated sense of self-worth had made her feel more comfortable around others found that others also felt at ease around her. She was now being chosen first or second in team games at recess instead of last. Once in a while someone is very direct and extra perceptive and says, "I feel better about myself, happier, more comfortable." Interestingly enough this same person will sometimes add, "But there are still areas of my life which I want to improve." Often the person with the *best* self-esteem can most easily face his or her liabilities.

Dr. Rollo May in his book *Man's Search for Himself* shows the inconsistency of feeling that God wants us to hate ourselves or demean ourselves in order to be "modest" or "humble."

> In the circles where self-contempt is preached, it is of course never explained why a person should be so ill-mannered and inconsiderate as to force his company on other people if he finds it so dreary and deadening himself. And furthermore the multitude of contradictions are never adequately explained in a doctrine which advises that we should hate the one self, "I," and love all others, with the obvious expectation that they will love us, hateful creatures that we are; or that the more we hate ourselves, the more we love God who made the mistake, in an off moment, of creating this contemptible creature, "I "[2]

Many people confuse the distinctions among *pride, humility,* and good *self-esteem.* The problem is not that self-esteem contradicts the Scriptures but rather that the words *pride* and *humility* are not correctly understood in the total light of Scripture.

Pride in the biblical sense involves a not-honest estimate of oneself. It means overrating one's worth. Sometimes it involves flaunting one's strengths against another supposedly weaker person. Often the person feels he or she can do quite well without God. Psalm 10:4 reads: "These wicked men, so proud and haughty, seem to think that God is dead. They wouldn't think of looking for him." Even those who accept their need for God can be pridefully involved in a self-righteous church clique. They may exclude other Christians because "they aren't like us socially" or brag about financial success, fame, or popularity, or even emphasize to some parent whose child has an IQ of 80 that their child just got a scholarship to Harvard or Yale. Pride, perhaps of the worst kind, can involve spiritual matters—claiming to have the best choir, the best pastor, or the most conversions of any church around when such is not true. Even if these evaluations are true, lauding it over others is an act of spiritual pride.

When I was in college, I really used to be threatened by friends who emphasized what a long quiet time they had each day or by those who were going to be missionaries and thought I too should be one. One man who was head of a missionary society actually told me: "Don't waste even two years teaching. You'll just come back to us then, and you will have wasted two years of your life!" I taught and counseled in schools for twelve years and not one year was wasted. Nor do I believe that I was ever meant to go to a foreign country or be in so-called full-time Christian work, at least not in the traditional meaning of that term. In my counseling and writing I am doing what I believe to be God's will for my life. I would not impose my professional life on someone else as though only what is right for me could be right for another person.

Spiritual pride is deadly, for it is more subtle than other forms of pride. The obnoxious woman in an office who constantly brags about her husband's important job or the couple who send out their yearly Christmas letter describing Suzie as top cheerleader for the third time and Joey as the star of his baseball team and Uncle Harvey as a multimillionaire who just loves to drop by have an obvious problem with pride. But the long public prayer in church or the person who is always promising to pray for you when you've just missed two Sunday services is harder to spot. Are they really genuine or are they showing spiritual pride? Sometimes only God knows.

Humility, on the other hand, is not some kind of wishy-washy self-hate. The person who claims that he is no good and that no one likes him may not necessarily be spiritual or humble; he may just not like himself. Compared to God we *are* nothing.

Christ says, "Yes, I am the Vine; you are the branches. Whoever lives in me and I in him shall produce a large crop of fruit. For apart from me you can't do a thing" (John 15:5).

The Bible clearly teaches that Christians are not to use their strong points to intimidate others. "Work happily together. Don't try to act big. Don't try to get into the good graces of important people but enjoy the company of ordinary folks" (Rom. 12:16). "Love each other with brotherly affection and *take delight in honoring each other*" (Rom. 12:10, italics mine). Yet some people seem to need to knock others down before they can feel worthwhile.

Real humility is simply an absence of concentration upon oneself. It means that while I like and accept myself I don't need to prove my worth excessively either to myself or to others. I am free to concentrate on the job of living.

In writing about the humble man, C. S. Lewis is really describing a person with a good self-image, for such an individual is the only one who would dare to be truly humble.

He will not be a sort of greasy, smarmy person, who is always telling you that, of course, he is nobody. Probably all you will think about him is that he took a real interest in what *you* said to *him*. If you do dislike him, it will be because you feel a little envious of anyone who seems to enjoy life so easily. He will not be thinking about humility: he will not be thinking about himself at all.[3]

Pride and false humility are just two possible symptoms demonstrated by the person with a low self-image. Irrational fears, depression, migraine headaches, colitis, hostility, sexual inadequacy, and other symptoms may also occur. Pride itself may at times be a defense for a very damaged ego. A person with an extremely low self-image can end up in a mental institution convinced that he or she is Napoleon. These people simply can't face who they are, and so they slip into an unreal world where they have worth and people recognize that worth.

Many become confused as to the *basis* for good self-esteem.

In a society where values are mixed this confusion becomes even greater. The person with material success, the one who "makes it" in this world, should feel good about his achievement *if* it was attained fairly and honestly. It is right to feel good about one's talents and successes. A child enjoys praise for high marks in school or commendation for being a good pitcher in Little League. Yet as adults too often we explain away our good cooking by saying "it was a simple recipe" or our business success by describing it as "a stroke of luck."

Worse still, while we sometimes have difficulty accepting compliments for our actions, we have an even harder time accepting feelings of worth about our inner selves. The Bible says that "Man looketh on the outward appearance but God looketh on the heart." The Bible emphasizes the value of the inner man. Motives, unseen effort, honesty, and caring are all qualities which should make a person feel good about himself. And certainly they are important in God's evaluation of a man.

The person who believes in a personal God has a supreme reason for affirming his or her self-worth—an all-powerful Being who cares, who loves, who even died for each human being. It is almost blasphemous to say that a human life is without worth when God values it so highly.

In short one could say that each person's worth becomes measurable by what he or she does with what he or she has. A man who had spent years in jail for child molesting (a crime which by the way is severely stigmatized even in prisons to the point that the life of such an offender is often in jeopardy) came to me for help. He said, "I still have the same impulses as before, but I want help so that I will never hurt anyone again." A heroin addict said, "I can't go on robbing in order to get a fix. I can't put my parents through anymore of this." Neither of these men had much. They were without money and jobs; society severely censured them; and psychologically they were very disturbed. But they tried harder than most people who don't have their temptations. For that effort I had great respect for their worth. Perhaps someday they will again have worth in a functional way in society. In a sense there are two branches of that quality we call self-worth: a person's value to others, to society; and his or her inner worth which is between an individual and God. Both are important, but God seems to put the highest value on the latter.

If a good self-image is conducive to a healthy handling of stress and is thus a preventative factor in psychosomatic illnesses, one could logically ask, "How does one acquire a good self-image?"

Within the first five or six years of life a child begins to develop the primary concept of his or her worth. He or she perceives this concept mainly from parents but also from relationships with other people. It is not surprising that the little girl whose mother tells her she's ugly grows up believing that untruth. Nor is it unusual that the child who thinks he's no good feels that way since his own father told me, "I really don't like my son and never have." But perhaps these examples are extreme. More subtle is the parent who frequently pushes his child aside and ignores him or the one who compares one child unfavorably to another.

In contrast, a woman I know went through a rough divorce proceeding when her child, Alice, was about four years old. Often when she became irritable she would start to take out her angry feelings on her daughter. Many times I heard her say things like, "I'm sorry I yelled at you, Alice. I'm upset right now, but it's not your fault and I love you very much." She was very conscious of Alice's needs to grow up liking Alice, and so it was almost predictable that Alice has grown up into a very self-assured adolescent.

However, more important for the purposes of this book is the fact that an adult self-image may be altered and reinforced by relationships with other people. If I have close relationships with people whom I can respect and who, in turn, respect me, then I am more likely to accept myself.

Not long ago a patient of mine said to me, "I like to be around you because you make me feel stronger even when we're not talking about problems." What she really meant, even though she didn't realize it, was that I have genuine respect for her which she senses, and my positive feelings about her make her stronger in that her self-esteem then goes up.

I once worked with some people who had a great many problems and who delighted in bickering and picking each other apart. It was a terribly negative atmosphere, and I grew increasingly unhappy. Yet when I would visit certain friends, the minute I walked into their home I felt better. The vibes were positive, toward themselves and toward me, and those vibes affected my self-image positively.

Friends who care, who tell you when you've done something well, who treat you as a person of value, reinforce your feelings of self-worth. And what could be more biblical when one considers the words of Christ: "You must love others as much as yourself" (Mark 12:31). True Christian love is one fundamental way to build one another's self-esteem, and such should be the result of Christian contacts in the church and in any Christian home and marriage. Paul urged husbands to "show the same kind of love to your wives as Christ showed to the church when he died for her" (Eph. 5:25). When this admonition is observed, marriage becomes an ego-building relationship.

Besides positive human relationships, responsible behavior also affects a person's self-image. If I behave in a way which I cannot respect, I will not like myself. The way out of such a dilemma is not to rationalize bad behavior but to change it. Not long ago I talked to a businessman who was having some rather severe emotional problems and who admittedly didn't like himself very much. He related incidents in which he had made "good business deals" by out-and-out cheating the people involved. He wanted to like himself, but he was living in such a dishonest way that self-acceptance was impossible. Before his feelings could change, his behavior had to change.

Even more common acts such as cutting someone out on the freeway, unnecessary abruptness on the telephone, lying to your children because it's easier, taking advantage of an insurance company on a settlement because "they have enough money," and just ignoring someone who needs you have an insidious effect in lowering your view of yourself. What do you most respect in other people? Be that yourself and you'll like yourself better.

A good self-image is an elusive quantity at times. We all know the feeling of having great security in one area and then facing another area with fear and turmoil. We all know too the fluctuations with which we accept ourselves. These probably depend on many factors: how responsible our behavior has been; the quality of our relationships; where we are physically; and perhaps many others.

But really to feel good and relaxed about oneself is a very safe, comfortable feeling; and safe, comfortable feelings minimize bad physical reactions.

Several years ago I was involved in taping a television show which included a panel discussion on drug abuse. All I had to do was sit there and perhaps speak if my courage grew sufficiently great. Yet I was nervous, my mouth was dry, my hands clammy, my stomach churning. I got through it—and even looked calm—but my body must have produced a lot of adrenalin that night for I was really frightened. Not long ago I faced another television interview. This time live, and this time an interview of only me. Before the program I wondered if I would go through the same agony again, but somehow the build-up ahead of time never hit. When I got to the studio, I was nervous but not terrified. To my absolute wonder, I actually enjoyed the interview! The interviewer was good, and so it was a fun experience. Right before I went on, I felt just nervous enough to try to be interesting, but I also had that wonderfully liberating feeling that the world would indeed go on if I failed! I had enough self-confidence to bear the thought of failure, which in a peculiar way helped me to succeed. Apart from some muscle tenseness I didn't get all the physical reactions this time that I had before. My body suffered less because my self-esteem was higher.

The unfortunate part about low self-esteem is that once it gets going it builds on itself. Failure breeds failure; self-hate breeds self-hate. And once the body starts reacting, that too starts a vicious cycle. When the body reacts very frequently, that is probably a pretty good indication of the need for some professional help. A low self-image makes it difficult to feel that a good God could love this bad person or that there could be any valid and important meaning in life. I have had people look at me with total disbelief when I expressed the feeling that their life had meaning. But perhaps even an awareness of the importance of a good self-image for psychological, physical, and spiritual health may be a step toward achieving that end.

It would seem that in the past the helping professions have overemphasized the effect of the mind on the body and underemphasized the importance of the physical and spiritual. But that fact does not mean that the mind does not play a tremendous role in the total health of the whole person. It is not the absence of stress but the correct handling of stress that will have a tremendous impact on the human body and spirit. In speaking of the stress of internment in a concentration camp, psychiatrist Viktor Frankl says:

> As for myself, when I was taken to the concentration camp of Auschwitz, a manuscript of mine ready for publication was confiscated. Certainly, my deep concern to write this manuscript anew helped me to survive the rigors of the camp. For instance, when I fell ill with typhus fever I jotted down on little scraps of paper many notes intended to enable me to rewrite the manuscript, should I live to the day of liberation. I am sure that this reconstruction of my last manuscript in the dark barracks of a Bavarian concentration camp assisted me in overcoming the danger of collapse.
>
> Thus it can be seen that mental health is based on a certain degree of tension, the tension between what one has already achieved and what one still ought to accomplish, or the gap between what one is and what one should become. Such tension is inherent in the human being and therefore is indispensable to mental well being.[4]

NOTES

1. Dr. Hans Selye, "Ideas for Living," *Family Circle*, July 1975, p. 46.

2. Rollo May, *Man's Search for Himself* (New York: W. W. Norton, 1953), p. 100.

3. C. S. Lewis, *Mere Christianity* (London: Collins Clear-Type Press, 1952), p. 112.

4. Viktor E. Frankl, *Man's Search for Meaning* (New York: Simon and Schuster, 1962), p. 106.

CHAPTER 5

————— • —————

A Spiritual Perspective

Margaret had been referred to me by her doctor when her frequent anxiety states began to take a physical toll. Her most recent tests showed the beginnings of an ulcer, and she was now on a bland diet and taking pills to relax her stomach.

A religious person, Margaret was active in church work and outwardly placid and happy. Yet she came across as a person who was rather mechanically going through the forms of being a Christian. She attended services of all churches, volunteered in the nursery on Sunday mornings, and sometimes visited the sick. But when she spoke of God, she did not seem deeply involved.

Then one afternoon she came in looking unusually happy and at peace with herself. "Last night I was reading a devotional book," she explained, "and suddenly it all made sense. I have been trying so hard to live my own life well that the very trying has made me uptight. So before I went to bed I committed my life fully to God. I told him that I could no longer run my life, that he could take over. After that," she continued, "I felt a peace I haven't known in months."

Over the few weeks that Margaret had been seeing me, she had made real concrete improvement. The combination of counseling and medical treatment had been effective. Yet after her new-found relationship with God, that recovery became even more rapid and complete. After a short while she was able to discontinue both the counseling sessions and the medical treatment. Her physician called it a "miraculous recovery." To me what occurred was a combination of physical, psychological, and spiritual help at an optimum level of effectiveness. But the final and, in this case, most significant help was spiritual.

The spiritual needs of persons have been overlooked too long by those in the behavioral sciences. Such ignorance is not valid even from an intellectual point of view. Elton Trueblood makes this point well:

> The fact that a great many people representing a great many civilizations and a great many centuries, and including large numbers of those generally accounted the best and wisest of mankind, have reported direct religious experience is one of the most significant facts about our world. The claim which their reports make is so stupendous and has been made in such a widespread manner that no philosophy can affort to neglect it. Since we cannot hope to build up a responsible conception of the universe unless we take into consideration every order of fact within it, the claim of religious experience with objective inference cannot be lightly dismissed. The very possibility that anything so important *might* be true gives our researches into these matters a necessary mood of seriousness. Since the claim is conceivably valid, there is the heaviest reproach upon those who fail to examine it seriously. When the claim is cavalierly rejected, without a careful examination, this is presumably because of some dogmatic position.[1]

From a psychological point of view psychiatrist Viktor Frankl has verbalized and promoted spiritual needs over and against the background of the relatively godless views of Freudian psychoanalysis. Frankl is not definitive regarding these spiritual needs, that is, he does not promote any specific religious thought, but rather explains them in terms of a person's need for meaning.

> Not every conflict is necessarily neurotic; some amount of conflict is normal and healthy. In a similar sense suffering is not always a pathological phenomenon; rather than being a symptom of neurosis, suffering may well be a human achievement, especially if the suffering grows out of existential frustration. I would strictly deny that one's search for a meaning

to his existence, or even his doubt of it, in every case is derived from, or results in, any disease. Existential frustration is in itself neither pathological nor pathogenic. A man's concern, even his despair, over the worthwhileness of life is a *spiritual distress* but by no means a *mental disease*. It may well be that interpreting the first in terms of the latter motivates a doctor to bury his patient's existential despair under a heap of tranquilizing drugs. It is his task, rather, to pilot the patient through his existential crises of growth and development.[2]

Frankl's acceptance of man's spiritual needs, in addition to those which are primarily psychological and physical, is further validated by what we know of even most primitive peoples. As far back as there is recorded history men and women have sought spiritual meaning for life. At times this search has ended in the worship of an animal or the sun or in the creation of an idol, carved with human hands. Our modern American culture is more sophisticated; yet how many of us make gods, inadequate as they may be, out of money, comfort, even our children? We have our god or gods because we need to reach out of ourselves to something or someone who will make our lives meaningful. Yet, while to seek meaning is healthy, finding that meaning in an unhealthy way can be destructive.

I saw a mother and a daughter for a short time who tragically pointed out this problem to me. Lois was a beautiful, bright child of eleven who was deeply disturbed emotionally. Her mother was alone, except for the child, and she idolized and doted upon this one object of her affections. As Lois showed some faint signs of improving, the mother panicked and jerked her out of counseling. She realized that as Lois got better they would grow somewhat apart, and she couldn't face that prospect. At the risk of her daughter's whole life, she withheld the possibility of treatment. Lois was her only form of meaning in this world, and what the mother refused to acknowledge was the very obvious fact that when the mother dies Lois will probably pay the extreme price of permanent hospitalization for her deep emotional problems.

The very opposite of this kind of sick satisfaction of one's needs is seen in the woman who found herself alone in a large city, except for a child to care for and a husband who was away on business trips at least half of the time. At first Mary found the situation intolerable. Yet she was wise enough to know that meaning for her life could not be found healthfully either in an overpossessiveness toward her child or in unreasonable demands upon her husband. She discovered that the local church needed help in their day-care program and became very active in helping disturbed teenagers who seemed instinctively drawn toward her. She tried psychotherapy and found some help there, but basically she needed meaning. To a large degree that need was met in her healthy involvement with the needs of others.

However, while Frankl's acknowledgment of a person's spiritual needs is gratifying, since it comes from a psychiatrist and puts the physical, spiritual, and psychological needs in perspective, his definition does not satisfy the Christian viewpoint. For the Christian perhaps St. Augustine still said it best when he wrote: "Thou madest us for Thyself and our heart is restless, until it repose in Thee." From the Christian point of view the need for spiritual fulfillment can only be satisfied in a relationship with Jesus Christ. When a person really comes to know Christ, it is as though he or she has found that previously unknowable factor that has always been missing.

A young missionary went deep into the Amazon area of South America and began to live and work with a small tribe of people who had never previously seen a white man. After many months of difficulty communicating as well as trusting, a young man in the tribe accepted Christ as the Lord and Master of his life. Quietly, he stared into the fire as he and the missionary sat outside his hut. Then he said, "Your God is the One whom my father sought and before him his father and his father. Now at last I have found him, but why did you not come before this?"

Thus while a person has a general need for meaning which seems more easily defined as spiritual rather than psychological, more specifically every individual needs a relationship with the God who says: "Before me there was no God formed, neither shall there be after me. I, even I, am the Lord; and beside me there is no saviour" (Isa. 43:10–11, KJV). The how of that relationship is perhaps shown as clearly in the New Testament Book of Romans as any other place in the Bible. "So now, since we have been made right in God's sight by faith in his promises, we can have real peace with him because of what Jesus Christ our Lord has done for us" (Rom. 5:1). "So there is now no condemnation awaiting those who belong to Christ Jesus. For the power of the life-giving Spirit—and this power is mine through Christ Jesus—has freed me from the vicious circle of sin and death. We aren't saved from sin's grasp by knowing the commandments of God, because we can't and don't keep them, but God put into effect a different plan to save us. He sent his own Son in a human body like ours—except that ours are sinful —and destroyed sin's control over us by giving himself as a sacrifice for our sins" (Rom. 8:1–3).

Despite what some Christians believe, being a Christian is not an insurance policy against emotional problems. Because Christianity does fill the void of meaninglessness that so many experience, Christians may have fewer difficulties in that direction. During the past few years I have seen a number of young people with drug problems. For many of them a large part of their dilemma has been what Frankl calls the "existential vacuum," the aching need for meaning. In a remarkable way Christ has been a large part of the answer for many of these young people. Their need has been more spiritual than psychological.

In an emotional crisis a Christian should be able to derive some help from his or her religious beliefs. There is a distinct danger, however, in spiritualizing emotional problems. For one thing, such an overemphasis may prevent a person from seeking professional help. He or she may experience excessive guilt feelings because of not being "a better Christian".

One woman in her late thirties came to see me when her depression became so acute that she could no longer deal with it. Her first comment was: "I shouldn't be here; if I were a better Christian, I wouldn't be depressed." Then she went out and bought a book which told her that all depression was sinful.

After that my progress in alleviating her guilt was basically ineffective. Finally she improved psychologically to the point where she could again bear the depression but was not yet fully recovered. Out of guilt she quit counseling and is continuing to struggle with a burden God never meant her to bear.

Rather than being the cause of guilt in the life of a Christian who has emotional problems, Christianity can be a dynamic, vital, healthy force in that person's life. As such it will have a positive effect spiritually, psychologically, and even physically.

In the first place, Christianity offers a sense of meaning to the problem of suffering. A middle-aged man who had some severe anxiety reactions took the more traditional view that his suffering must be God's punishment for his past sins. When he started counseling, he was angry about his suffering and felt a sense of futility over the problem of pain. "Maybe I should give up," he said. "I've tried all sorts of therapy, and all I feel is guilt over how bad I must be for God to give me this much pain." His spiritual view of himself as someone whom God was angry at just lowered his already low self-esteem and increased his anxiety. The greater his anxiety became, the greater his sense of worthlessness. His spiritual and emotional sides were effectively destroying each other until they became almost indistinguishable.

After a number of sessions he came into my office one day and said: "I can now see meaning in all of this suffering, for it has given me a sensitivity and compassion for the pain of others that I didn't have before. And knowing that there can be good coming out of this has reduced my anger and fear to the point where I actually am beginning to feel less psychological pain."

He has begun to learn that his psychological problems are not spiritual, in the sense of his being sinful or being under the wrath of an angry God. He now views God as someone who loves him and is willing to help him, a viewpoint which elevates his self-image.

Christianity offers a sense of self-worth to its followers even though this is clearly *not* the teaching of many Christians. Indeed one of the most difficult problems I encounter as a Christian counselor is negative Christians who present the teachings of Christ in a distorted fashion. As I told one teenager the other day, "Please don't turn away from God because well-meaning Christians are using his teachings as a weapon to make you feel guilty. God probably disagrees with them as much as you do because this is *not* biblical Christianity!" This boy really wanted to know God and needed spiritual fulfillment, but he was being condemned by Christians because of his hair, clothes, friends, and other relatively superficial things. In the name of Christianity, he was made to feel worthless.

In contrast was the teenager who told her mother she wanted to smoke cigarettes but "knew" her mother would condemn her. Without overspiritualizing the problem, Debbie's mother said she hoped Debbie wouldn't smoke because smoking was injurious to one's health. Then unpredictably her mother suggested that Debbie go and get the package of cigarettes that she had bought and try them. Surprised, Debbie did so and hated them. Without the temptation of forbidden fruits, Debbie gave up the idea of smoking, and it never became a roadblock between her and God. She was not criticized by her mother nor did she feel rejected by God. Her interest in God continues, and she views him as Someone who cares about her and who wants to be involved in her life.

Such a view of God does not imply a watered-down sense of morality. Debbie came to see me the other day with the question, "How can I know at school when I'm doing what God wants or not? Sometimes things happen so fast that I'm not sure." She really wanted answers, not so much out of guilt and fear, but out of love for God whom she has come to know. While there are some things she chooses not to do because she is a Christian, her stand on these issues only increases her image of herself. She respects herself for her honesty, for her refusal to hurt people, for not getting loaded at parties. Furthermore she feels accepted and loved by God and therefore feels a sense of worth because of that relationship. Partly because of her mother's wisdom, she has not turned against God. One is reminded of the quote from Nietzsche: "Maybe I would have believed in a

Redeemer if the Christians had looked more redeemed." A cop-out? Maybe. But perhaps this feeling partially explains many people's reactions to God.

Those who lived in New Testament times and participated in the early church did not as a whole go around demeaning people. When Christ saw the group ready to stone the woman caught in adultery, he did not join them. He pointed out their sin, and they quietly turned and left. Left alone with the woman, Christ asked, "Where are your accusers? Didn't even one of them condemn you?"

"No, sir," she said.

And Jesus said, "Neither do I. Go and sin no more" (John 8:10–11).

Christ acknowledged that what she had done was sinful, but he didn't pound her into the ground with guilt. She didn't need that; she was already down enough. Yet the religious leaders of the day wanted her executed and said to Christ, "Moses' law says to kill her. What about it?" (John 8:4).

Jesus asked for water from a woman at a well, and "The woman was surprised that a Jew would ask a 'despised Samaritan' for anything—usually they wouldn't even speak to them!—and she remarked about this to Jesus.

"He replied, 'If you only knew what a wonderful gift God has for you, and who I am, you would ask me for some *living* water!" (John 4:7–10).

Jesus goes on very gently to point out her sin: "For you have had five husbands, and you aren't even married to the man you're living with now" (John 4:18). He does not condone sin, but he is not harsh. Consequently, the woman went out and told everyone: "Come and meet a man who told me everything I ever did! Can this be the Messiah?" (John 4:28–29).

Christ lifted up people; he did not crush them. More than anyone else, he knew the fragileness of the human ego. Only toward those who were religious snobs, those who went around berating others, particularly those who were already down, did Christ show strong anger. "Yes, woe upon you, Pharisees, and you other religious leaders—hypocrites! For you tithe down to the last mint leaf in your garden, but ignore the important things —justice and mercy and faith" (Matt 23:23).

In this day, too, Christ gives a sense of worth to those who are related to him. In the redemptive act, God takes the form of man and is offered as a sacrifice in payment for man's sin. This implies a tremendous unprecedented concern for each member of the human race. God loves me! An astounding thought! A personal God gives life meaning and imputes to people a sense of importance. On the other hand, for some people God is a remote deity who simply started this thing we call life and left it. Still others contend that God does not exist at all (which seems intellectually difficult to accept). To adhere to either of these latter viewpoints makes the person and life itself seem too fleeting to be accorded much importance.

Mark Twain, best known for his humor and local color, wrote a seldom read passage at the end of *The Mysterious Stranger*. He relates a conversation between Satan and a little boy. Says Satan: "It is true, that which I have revealed to you; there is no God, no universe, no human race, no earthly life, no heaven, no hell. It is all a dream—a grotesque and foolish dream. Nothing exists but you. And you are but a *thought*—a vagrant thought, a useless thought, a homeless thought, wandering forlorn among the empty eternities".

Then says the little boy: "He vanished, and left me appalled; for I knew, and realized, that all he had said was true."[3]

Far-fetched? Perhaps. But somehow in spite of *Tom Sawyer* and *Huckleberry Finn* this passage may represent where Mark Twain lived within his own mind. And realistically it is perhaps not far from expressing emptiness when life without God is carried to its logical extreme.

Even in the middle of deep problems, however, the person who knows God should feel a sense of worth and meaning. As one of my patients said, "Now that I know it is right to like myself, when I feel down, I ask God for a better self-image and also for the wisdom to know how to develop it." Her self-esteem may not always be high, but at least she no longer resists liking herself and enjoys feelings of self-worth when they occur.

One of the ways that Christianity can help build a healthy self-image in a person is through contributing to the development of good relationships—both with God and with other people. Ideally, a good relationship with God tends to improve the level of our relationships with others.

A year ago my father died from a massive stroke. Before the funeral I was calm and felt a deep sense of the meaning of eternal life. Yet there is something gross about some of the death symbols in our society which militates against such a feeling. Purposely, I did not see my father after his death because I preferred remembering him alive. Partly at my request, the casket was closed at the service, but the family was ushered into a tiny room right up by the casket. As I looked at that heavy box which contained the remains of one who a few weeks before had given no evidence of being near death, a sense of bleakness and loneliness hit me. I began to cry, quietly but rather uncontrollably for me.

Nothing and no one on this earth could have helped me at that moment, but I knew I had to get myself together. I forced my glance away from the casket and looked at the flowers. There were several beautiful red poinsettias which looked anything but deathlike. Then with a sudden wave of awareness I realized on a deep emotional level, not just with my head, that my father was not really there. He was already with God. Of course, his body was still in the casket. But I knew at that moment that my father would have echoed the words of Paul: "We are not afraid, but are quite content to die, for then we will be at home with the Lord" (2 Cor. 5:8).

After that I could almost rejoice in where he was rather than falling apart over the symbols of death around me. I felt a closeness to God and a calm that had no completely human explanation. At the graveside a couple of friends were upset because they didn't know what to do or say. I was able to impart a sense of my peace to them, and our relationship became closer as a result. At the end of a very hard day, made easier by relationships with God and others, I had a good sense of self-worth. I cannot draw a line between my emotional strength, my relationship with God, and my friendships; each entered in. But I do know that my Christian relationships God-ward and person-ward helped me, not only to get through the day, but to do it more comfortably and with a good feeling about myself.

Unlike many of my professional colleagues, I believe a relationship with God is something concrete, not just a good psychological feeling. Prayer is psychologically uplifting, but it is also real communication with a real God.

In *Beyond Our Selves* Catherine Marshall relates an incident from the writings of Dr. A. B. Simpson, a New York clergyman. In his twenties Dr. Simpson developed a debilitating heart problem which made his ministry very difficult.

> Usually it took him until Wednesday to get over the effects of his Sunday sermons. Climbing stairs or even a slight elevation was suffocating agony.
>
> Dr. Simpson was only thirty-seven when he was told by his physician that he might not have long to live. On his doctor's advice, he went for a long rest to the resort town of Old Orchard Beach, Maine. There he happened into an unusual religious meeting conducted by a Boston physician, Dr. Charles Cullis. Dr. Cullis was then having much success with treating tubercular patients through prayer and common sense health measures alone.
>
> Several statements made in the meeting about healing through prayer sent Dr. Simpson back to the Bible to find out what Jesus had to say on the subject. He soon became convinced that Jesus had always meant for His gospel to include healing of the body along with healing of the mind and the spirit.
>
> In the quiet of his room, Dr. Simpson reviewed his life. He was always struggling desperately for even his minimal needs —for enough health to keep going, for enough ideas and intellectual resources to write talks and sermons, for enough caring about other people. It was almost as if his creed was "Of myself I must do everything." But somehow he always fell short of his objectives. Was God now trying to reach him with a new idea? Had he ever really given God a chance to run his life?

One Friday afternoon shortly after that, Dr. Simpson went for a walk. Since he was always out of breath, he was forced to walk slowly. The path led into a pine wood, and he sat down on a fallen log to rest. All around him was that thick carpet of moss so often seen in the Maine woods. Sunlight filtered through the tall pines, laying striped patterns across the emerald green floor. Simpson pulled out his watch and saw that it was three o'clock.

"All things in my life looked dark and withered," Simpson wrote afterward. "The doctors had made it clear that they could do nothing for me. Intellectual life and spiritual life were also at a low ebb. So there in the woods I asked God to become my life for me, including physical life for all the needs of my body until my life work was done. And I solemnly promised to use His spiritual and physical strength in me for the good of others. God was there all right, because every fiber of my body was tingling with His Presence. He had come to meet me at the point of my helplessness."

A few days later, Simpson took a long hike and climbed a mountain three thousand feet high. "When I reached the mountaintop," he related joyously, "the world of weakness and fear was lying at my feet. From that time I literally had a new heart in my breast."[4]

After this experience Simpson lived a vigorous life, wrote and preached continually, and died at the age of seventy-six.

There are those who would psychologize such an experience, for the human mind has difficulty comprehending a concrete relationship with God. Yet is not God by definition somewhat incomprehensible? If God cannot touch a human body in a divine manner, then he in essence becomes something less than God. The obscurity of his power along with its reality is one of the proofs of God's existence, for if I as a finite being understood God completely, God would not be God.

However, God's capacity for divine intervention in human lives does not guarantee that intervention. People do not need to feel ignored by God and sinful if they remain chronically ill or if a certain problem persists in their life. Sometimes it is those whom God can trust the most that suffer the most. But with that suffering God gives compensations, for God is no man's debtor.

A silversmith was asked to describe the process of refining silver. He explained that silver is refined by exposing it to heat, each time at a greater intensity than before. The intensity of the heat toward the end of the process is far greater than at the outset, for at the beginning such strong heat would ruin the silver. During the times that the silver is in the fire, the silversmith never leaves it, for it must be watched closely. When asked how he knew when the refining process was complete, the silversmith replied: "When I can see my image in it."

Something of this same process occurs in the life of the Christian who develops a vital relationship with God. He or she is truly being made into the image of God. Pain is never meaningless for the Divine Silversmith stays with a person and uses it to make the person more like God.

And for the person who knows God in this way there are dramatic results in terms of his or her relationships with others. Not long ago I read a book which spoke specifically to my own deep feelings and needs. The author seemed to have a profound insight into people's emotions and even their suffering. Later I had the privilege of meeting her, an encounter which was not without great curiosity on my part. She was a bubbly, happy person but not superficial. I felt her depth, but I did not know where it came from until I later discovered that she had been hospitalized with tuberculosis for three years. Her suffering had not made her into a dull, depressing person; quite to the contrary, she had been drawn closer to God and had grown to resemble him more completely. It is impossible to suffer and remain the same. People either become bitter or they change into more compassionate, gentle human beings.

To those who say that God is for people who have nothing else going for them in life, I refer them to a woman like this author-friend. She has a lot going for her, both in her career and in her family, but the beautiful part is that her suffering was not a wasted portion of life. It too had meaning.

When one looks around at the suffering in this world, what sense is there to human life if that suffering is meaningless? Although Americans seem to idolize pleasure, there is more pain and monotony in this world than happiness and pleasure. It would seem only logical that a person's explanation of life would have to take suffering into account.

If there is one key which most completely opens the door between any human being and the kind of meaningful relationship with God which we have spoken about, it is the key of commitment. Commitment means more than Christ as my Sin-Bearer. It means that all I am, down to the most intimate core, belongs to him. It means risk, for it involves leaving decisions and outcomes to him.

When I began my practice as a family counselor and had written my first book, I felt that I had not only discovered an area of functioning which was divinely appointed for me, but I knew that I was doing what I really wanted. Yet somehow as one gets that which one wants very much, there is a tendency to hold on tightly and take back things which were originally committed to God.

One Sunday afternoon I became aware that this was precisely what I was doing. I wanted God to own every part of me, and yet I was afraid that if I gave everything back to him I might lose something. All afternoon and evening I evaluated the possibilities until I became convinced that the truest way to have meaning in my life was to give God back each part of it. My counseling practice and my writing were among the hardest to relinquish. Yet within a year God blessed that *commitment* by doubling both. God is, after all, a god of love, and he does not take things away from us unless he can give us something better. Our only problem is that sometimes we don't see with God's perspective, and so we have no real guarantee regarding the things we commit to him.

Commitment is not a one-time thing. It is a moment-by-moment process which needs constant maintenance. But it is only through complete commitment that we develop a close relationship with God. Then he has the greatest opportunity really to operate in our lives. My own experience along this line is best expressed in a poem:

When gently from my tight, clenched hands
God took of earthly things which I held dear,
Confused, His love I did not understand;
I grasped still more, lest more should disappear.

But yet in love He took until to Him alone
   I turned, for all else seemed
Unsteady, apt to fade; reluctant, still
I gave to Him the things I precious deemed.

He took, but then He gladly gave first of Himself,
   His love, His joy, and rest;
Until it seemed the things which I had saved
Were worthless toys compared to heaven's best.

Then, while with willing, open hands
I held all earthly gifts for Him to see
And take or give, apart from my demands,
He gave me back the things He took from me.[5]

When the Christian life becomes a daily relationship with a living God, it ceases to be a negative experience. To be a Christian demands a certain level of morality and standards which is conducive to good self-esteem. But the emphasis is on the positive, not the "Thou shalt nots." One young girl said to me, "I wish I weren't a Christian so that I could do what is good for me." That is Christianity all backwards.

Christ in me means life with greater potential, meaning, and power than ever before. A young lady sat in my office not long ago with a story of some rather traumatic negative experiences with Christian friends. She was very tense and frightened; yet I had little chance to be reassuring because she needed almost the entire hour to explain her situation. As I looked at her at the end of our time, I said, "What you have told me is something that will require more than this one hour to get through. But meanwhile, try to forget some of the negative past and concentrate on God's love and power, for he does love you in the middle of all of this confusion." To my surprise, some of the tension disappeared from her face, and she replied, "Thank you. That helps already." She needed to see a loving God. She, like the woman at the well, had already heard enough of what she should and shouldn't do. She needed considerable help to begin to view God differently, but even the simple statement that God loved her seemed to give her a glimmer of hope.

To know God with complete abandon is the greatest challenge of the Christian life. Once a person walks in total commitment to God, he or she unlocks the door to all sorts of possibilities, for God is then free to work through his or her life.

In an older hymn, Dr. A. B. Simpson wrote the refrain, "I take . . . He undertakes." *Our* responsibility is a life fully given to God. The resources for that life are *his* responsibility. This means that Christ in me can do everything. "I can do all things through Christ which strengtheneth me" (Phil. 4:13, KJV). We tend to try to live so independently of God at times when all along God is willing to undertake for us if we will but take. Ours is the first move, for God operates within the realm of our free choice.

A person is not all spirit any more than he or she is all mind or all body, but the spiritual side is a very real dimension and has great potential for power and fulfillment.

NOTES

1. Elton Trueblood, *Philosophy of Religion*, (New York: Harper, 1957).

2. Viktor E. Frankl, *Man's Search for Meaning* (New York: Clarion, 1972), pp. 104, 105.

3. Mark Twain, *The Mysterious Stranger, American Heritage*, ed. Leon Howard, Louis B. Wright, and Carl Bode (Boston: D. C. Heath and Co., 1955), 2: 550.

4. Catherine Marshall, *Beyond Our Selves* (New York: Avon Books, 1968), pp. 162–64.

5. Elizabeth Skoglund, *Decision* (Minneapolis: Billy Graham Evangelistic Association, 1967), pp. 28–29.

————— • —————

CHAPTER 6

When Christians Need Help

The first time I saw Carlos Sanchez was at a high-school assembly. At that time I was still with the schools, doing group counseling with tenth-graders. Our new school building was incomplete, and so we had no auditorium. Therefore, eighteen hundred of us were seated outside on bleachers under what seemed a hundred degrees of hot blazing sun. It was difficult to see against the strong sunlight, and the voices of the various speakers seemed to fade into the expanse of space on the football field.

Then Carlos was introduced: young, in his twenties, Chicano, nervous but sincere. "There are two words you will hear today," he proclaimed in a sharp, loud voice that seemed to penetrate the air: "Jesus Christ and the Bible."

Having thoroughly captured his audience by the force of his voice and by that unexpected statement, he went on to tell of his background in a middle-class, respectable home. Then he described his first experiments with drugs at age twelve until he had finally run the gamut of available drugs and ended up a heroin addict.

Three years ago he had gone to visit his sister to ask for money with which he meant to buy a fix. She said that if he would first read a book she had about God, she would give him the money he wanted. But after reading the book, Carlos forgot about the money and his fix. Later he committed his life to Christ, and he was profoundly changed.

Now at this school assembly we met and felt a common bond. Carlos was effectively helping teenagers on drugs, some of the same teenagers I was counseling. Yet he had a vast experience which I envied.

We had lunch and talked. Then we pooled our efforts and for months had a direct combined influence on a large number of teenage drug users. He had such a dramatic experience with God that I felt at first a little defensive. After all, my background had been pretty sheltered. I had never smoked a joint or gotten drunk. And I certainly had not seen God perform the kind of dramatic miracles in my life that Carlos had seen in his.

Yet in the back of my mind grew the gnawing, uneasy feeling that all was not right. Carlos had no social life, except kids who needed him twenty-four hours a day. He began to show signs of fatigue; he mentioned God less and less. And from the beginning he seemed obsessed with proving to the establishment, who had denigrated Carlos the Addict, that Carlos the Speaker, Counselor, and Christian was indeed a man to be respected.

And respected he was by adults and kids alike. Indeed he had an intuitive sense of how to approach teenagers in trouble. They listened to him while those of us who watched learned more from him about counseling than we had learned in many college courses.

Fourteen months later he was dead from an overdose of barbiturates. This driven man had done great things and had shown great potential, but he *was* driven. In spite of his spiritual outlook and the powerful effect that God had on his life, his own low sense of self-esteem, combined perhaps with some biochemical factors, had driven him to a desperate act. I have often wondered if he wouldn't have been alive today if psychotherapy and medical help had been combined with his spiritual experiences.

People often seem to wonder what the counseling process is all about. Some ask if they should lie on a couch, or if I take notes, or if I want a detailed family history. They ask about dreams, hypnosis, and wonder if ten years of problems will be corrected in one or two sessions. At a first session they are sometimes apprehensive, then relieved, and then partially confused when the setting seems so casual and normal. It's as though they expect a kind of mystical atmosphere in which a magic wand will wave away their problems. Perhaps part of their confusion lies in the variety of methods which are employed.

Most common to the American public is the typical television presentation of analysis, conducted by a psychotherapist seated near a couch on which a patient reclines and explores his own feelings out loud. At some point the patient gains insight into his problems, and his symptoms quickly disappear. The therapist usually looks a little strange and frequently seems to remain aloof during the whole process. Such an image of psychotherapy is neither fair to the field in general nor probably to Freud's concept of psychoanalysis. Yet the emphasis on insight into the past and on the aloofness of the therapist accurately characterizes essential components of psychoanalysis. While some of Freud's understandings of human behavior are invaluable to psychotherapy, basically psychoanalysis seems to have been lacking in adequate success, is very lengthy and expensive, and has been replaced in many instances by newer forms of therapy. While psychoanalytic techniques are still used by many counselors, it is no longer fair to assume that psychoanalysis and psychotherapy are necessarily synonymous.

Behavior Modification, for example, emphasizes a desensitizing or deconditioning process to rid patients of symptoms such as irrational fear of heights or elevators. Tapes may be used or even hypnosis.

Reality Therapy is concerned with the concept of responsibility, a word which is defined in broad terms, and aims toward developing greater self-esteem. *Logotherapy* has a number of various facets, such as the use of paradoxical intention in getting rid of fears and obsessions, but is more directly concerned with the concept of a life-meaning which is unique for each person.

Other schools of thought ranging from *Gestalt Therapy* or *Primal Therapy* to a vast myriad of group therapies are prevalent today. It takes some research and thought for a person to find what is right for him, and no one should blame the whole counseling field because of one off-beat experience. In the various types of available counseling much is good, some is bad, and probably a great deal is neutral and ineffective.

Common to a good counseling experience, regardless of the technique, is the relationship between the counselor and patient. According to psychiatrist William Glasser:

> . . . *at the time any person comes for psychiatric help he is lacking the most critical factor for fulfilling his needs, a person whom he genuinely cares about and who he feels genuinely cares about him.* Sometimes it is obvious that the patient has no close relationships. Many times, however, especially in patients who are functioning fairly well and come to a psychiatrist in private practice, the lack of involvement is not apparent. Patients may have devoted wives, friends, and family, but they still are unable to fulfill their needs. Despite the presence of people who claim they care, the patient is either not able to accept their love, or he does not care for them. What appear to be satisfactory relationships are not satisfactory for him, a condition often graphically illustrated by the case of many suicides. A person who commits suicide may have many people who care about him and he may be successful in his work, yet still leave a note describing the overwhelming loneliness and isolation he feels. Therefore, to obtain help in therapy the patient must gain or regain involvement, first with the therapist and then with others.[1]

The basis of a good relationship between counselor and patient lies in the quality of empathy. Empathy is different from sympathy in that it shares in the person's experience but does not feel sorry for the person in any kind of weakening way. Sympathy is destructive, for it says, "You are really in bad shape, someone to be pitied, even someone who may not make it." It sometimes implies, "You have a right to be weak or give up since life has treated you so harshly."

A young girl who had been hospitalized for months in multiple braces deeply resented the sympathy she felt when she left the hospital. People looked pityingly at her and told her how sorry they were for her. She had never felt that way in the hospital, for there the atmosphere was completely different. People outside sometimes felt that the patients treated one another cruelly. In fact, the patients did exhibit a rather tough attitude. If a person complained because he or she couldn't stand, a typical retort was: "What do you mean you can't stand? She can't sit." There was a close, cooperative helping spirit but never the weakening effect of sympathy.

In contrast to sympathy, empathy says, "I understand how you feel, I really hear where you're at, but I think you're worth enough to be able to handle it." A while back as I talked to a young college student I could feel his frustration. When he described the end of the school year approaching with its deadlines for research papers and final exams, I remembered my own college years and my recurring nightmare in which I hadn't read the assigned text and thus failed to pass the final exam and graduate. I had forgotten that dream until then.

I could feel the exhaustion of his long hours at work, the social pressures which were impinging from his girl friend and football friends, and I sensed his fear that failure in one area or another was simply inescapable. This was empathy.

Had I fostered his tendency to feel sorry for himself, to feel that life had given him a rough deal, he would have been weakened by our contact. But to feel that he was understood by someone who knew his efforts and respected them imparted a sense of worth to him.

Essential to an appreciation of that empathy is a relationship of trust. When I asked one woman what was different in her relationship with her therapist which made it unique, her first answer was, "Trust." When I asked her to explain, she replied: "I never felt I could tell my mother something that she would keep to herself. I knew she would tell someone." She went on to explain that with her counselor she knew that what she said was safe and that, furthermore, with him she was really heard. When she said that she hurt, he believed her. When she tried and failed, he believed that she had tried. He heard what she said, and she could say anything.

A little girl came home from the park in tears because she couldn't hit the baseball. Worse than that, she ended up being the last one chosen to be on a team because she really doesn't play ball well.

As she threw herself on her bed, she said to her mother, "I'm just no good at baseball. I'm no good at anything."

In an attempt to be overreassuring her mother replied: "Jodie, that's not true. You're good at everything." When Jodie got almost hysterical and screamed, "You don't understand," the mother was thoroughly confused.

Later when Jodie and I were talking, she told me how bad she was at baseball. She also said she was stupid—and then proceeded to describe various books she had read, using very adult words.

When I agreed that she probably wasn't very good at baseball, she seemed relieved. She had been heard. Furthermore, she then heard me in return when I offered her concrete reasons why I thought she was a very bright little girl. Because I could admit her weaknesses, she could accept my evaluation of her strengths.

At another time I heard a young man say as he left my office, "Man! This is neat! You can say anything you want in there and you don't get put down. You can be you and not worry about what people think."

Such longings for a trusting, open relationship seem to be universal. In 1852 the English poet Matthew Arnold wrote the following words during the Victorian period of English history when thoughts and feelings were not freely expressed:

> I knew the mass of men concealed
> Their thoughts, for fear that if revealed
> They would by other men be met
> With blank indifference, or with blame reproved;
> I knew they lived and moved
> Tricked in disguises, alien to the rest
> Of men, and alien to themselves—and yet
> The same heart beats in every human breast![2]

Continues Arnold:

> Ah! well for us, if even we,
> Even for a moment, can get free
> Our heart, and have our lips unchained;
> For that which seals them hath been deep ordained![3]

In a good counseling relationship the heart and lips can become unchained, and the fact that a person can do that and still be accepted and respected is in itself deeply therapeutic. In a way the trust that is present in a good counseling session amounts to becoming psychologically naked and then finding out that you still have worth.

The relationship that accepts and cares is also one which in a sense teaches. Many of my patients who have had previous counseling experiences complain that they only sat and talked in a sort of monologue with almost no response from the counselor. This nondirective approach is, of course, part of one whole school of thought in psychotherapy. To many patients, however, it is frustrating and relatively unproductive. In my opinion, part of the counseling relationship involves a two-way communication in which the counselor objectifies situations and offers suggestions. It is not a dominant ordering of another's life, however. For example, suggesting that involvement with a married person can be destructive psychologically and spiritually is a valid observation and seems an appropriate observation for a counselor to make under certain circumstances. As I looked at a thirty-year-old woman who had just painfully extricated herself from such a situation, I rather bluntly said: "Please don't do that again!" Her reaction was positive, both in agreeing with my statement and in being pleased that I cared enough to be blunt.

People often need to see that others' rejection of them is not really due to their inadequacy but to a problem which the other person has, like the father who dislikes his daughter because he wanted a son. Others need suggestions on how to handle anger responsibly or how to accept criticism at work or even how to budget their income. These practical aspects of counseling are all part of the caring that should be involved.

For those who have not had any counseling, or who have not been in a good therapeutic situation, that relationship is hard to portray. Perhaps the bluntness of children shows it best.

A little girl who has been torn apart by broken home relationships tested me for months to see if I too would abandon her. One day after I thought we had developed a pretty good rapport, Jenny came into my office in a very grumpy mood. In answer to my question of what was wrong, she said, "I don't want to be here." Surprised, I asked why. In reply she became quite verbal. "Because I want you to be at my house, to be my parent. I don't want to just come here. I want you to meet everyone I know, even my cat, and then I'll be happy." That day she left the office very slowly, a step at a time with several good-bys, ending with, "Good-by, Second Mother." In a way it was sad that she wanted more of me than I could give her, but for a child who had seemingly never trusted anyone, it was a start toward good mental health.

Some months later Jenny came in with a very quiet, almost disturbed look on her face. For a month or two she had been doing so well that both her parents and I had felt that she was probably ready to discontinue therapy or at least taper off. But she had steadfastly refused that suggestion. This day she remained aloof. Then finally she burst out: "Would you really understand and not be hurt if I said something?" After some reassurance, she continued: "I don't think I need you anymore. But I do like you," she added quickly. We agreed to stop counseling, but I had the feeling that she still felt I had interpreted her action as a rejection of me. Later in the week I wrote her a note saying that I had thought of her when her appointment time came around but was so happy that she could spend the afternoon playing with her friends. Later her mother called and told me that after the note Jenny was sure that I still cared and that I wasn't hurt. Since then, Jenny has done very well on her own.

A teenager described her relationship to her counselor more

succinctly: "I feel I kind of carry you around with me and together we can make it." Then a few weeks later, "I still need to see you and talk, but somehow now I tend to feel I'm doing things more by myself. It's more scary this way—but better because I feel more whole."

A good counseling relationship is close, caring, open—and *real*. I once saw a cartoon showing a sign above a psychiatrist's door which read: "Love for sale." It told only a small part of truth, for in any good counseling relationship there is genuine feeling and a true extending of oneself. Some are in it only for money, but then there are those in every profession.

In talking about the counseling relationship psychiatrist Rollo May gives the following eloquent description:

> It raises the prestige of the one who is understood, and helps give him a sense of worth as a person. This understanding breaks down the barriers which separate a man from his fellows, it draws the other human being for a moment out of the loneliness of his individual existence and welcomes him into community with another soul. It is like inviting the traveler in from his snowy and chilly journey to warm himself for an hour before the fire on another's hearth. Such understanding, it is not too much to say, is the most objective form of love. That is why there is always a tendency on the part of the counselee to feel some love toward the counselor, this person "who understands me." There are few gifts that one person can give to another in this world as rich as understanding.[4]

In addition to confusion over *what* counseling is all about, many people genuinely do not know *why* people seek professional psychological help. Some think you have to be crazy or weird. Actually most crazy or psychotic individuals wouldn't walk into a private counseling office on their own. More likely it's the person who wants to live more comfortably who seeks professional help.

A couple came to me not long ago because they felt that their marriage was headed for trouble and they wanted to prevent it.

A little boy was brought to me because he was too shy and therefore other children picked on him. An elderly lady came because she wanted help in building a meaningful life now that her children were raised. A businessman wanted help in his interpersonal relationship at work. None of these people was weird or strange. Indeed, they were probably less so than most people one meets walking down the street!

Some people seek help with far deeper problems than those just listed. But again, rather than being strange they are often people whom one must respect greatly for the struggle and effort which they are exerting against great odds.

Michelle, a woman of twenty-five, had been abandoned by her parents when she was four, shunted through ten foster homes in the course of growing up, and then left by her husband for another woman. She finally resorted to an overdose of pills in order to escape a life which had shown her little but pain. By the time I saw her, she was ready to try. Far from thinking less of her for attempting suicide, I could only feel tremendous admiration for her efforts to put life together.

In spite of the valid reasons people seek counseling, many consider it something to be resisted and, if possible, hidden. Somehow to most people physical pain is acceptable while psychological agony is not. It is all right to say, "My tooth aches," but not "My heart is breaking." It is noble to keep working with a stuffy nose or a sore throat, but it is just expected that you will keep on functioning when you're depressed or anxious.

A young woman was carried from her job when she passed out and couldn't be revived. Everyone thought she had a heart attack, and bitter, angry remarks were made against her husband who recently had been giving her a bad time. Plans were made to make her workload easier, and friends thought of things to do for her children so that she could rest more.

Then the final diagnosis was announced—tachycardia (rapid pulse) due to overwork and tension. In essence, a physical problem had been created by psychological stress. Immediately, interest waned. "She's just going to have to pull herself together," some said. Others compared their own home lives to hers and felt that their situation wasn't any better. In general, compassion evaporated when the diagnosis became psychological.

Even within the area of psychological ills we've somehow managed to divide things neatly into the acceptable and the unacceptable. It's okay to be grief stricken and incapacitated *briefly* during a bereavement. But don't extend that pain too far beyond the funeral, or you'll be accused of indulging in self-pity. If your husband leaves you for another woman, which may hurt more than a bereavement, you may be told to go out and show him that you're not going to waste time being upset over him. Inner feelings of rejection and hurt are not tolerated nearly as easily as pain resulting from job loss or a catastrophic illness. Nor is prolonged pain acceptable.

We all tend to project on others our concept of pain. What hurts me, hurts you. What doesn't hurt me, shouldn't hurt you. And if you suffer when I think you should not, then my tendency is to look down on you as a weak person. The stigma of psychotherapy is a result of this tendency. People who have never suffered from a divorce or a child on drugs or from a childhood background which shattered a sense of good self-worth sometime feel that those who have these problems should "not give in to them" or "should just forget them and go on." Some who have a severe fear or phobia of snakes or black spiders feel amazingly justified; yet in some illogical way they ridicule a friend who may have the same irrational fear of an elevator or freeway. Worse still, others like an alcoholic, for example, who beats his children and loses job after job looks down on an alcoholic friend who seeks professional help because he wants to handle his problem more responsibly. Somehow there is the feeling that if you don't admit you have a problem you really don't have one. And going to a counselor is an admission of need.

Christians have their own additional reasons for resisting counseling. Many identify Freud with an attitude of godlessness, and Freud and psychoanalysis are their only counseling reference points. In actuality, current psychological techniques are neither all Freudian nor all godless.

Other Christians feel that God is the whole answer for psychological problems. They confused the spiritual with the psychological.

"Some of you spend forty-five dollars a week for a psychiatrist when without cost you could simply trust God." So concluded the Sunday morning service. The congregation slowly filed out, some feeling a twinge of guilt over their weekly psychotherapy sessions, others wondering why they still had problems when they were really trying so hard to trust God.

What the clergyman in this case failed to recognize is that counseling is not meant to be a substitute for God. It is intended to be a help in meeting psychological needs, just as pastoral counseling should help a person spiritually and medical treatment corrects physical ailments. All three areas overlap and interact, but each is also distinct.

The need of counseling should never be interpreted disparagingly. Nor should that need imply a lack of trust in God. Rather, God may well use the counseling process as a tool in a person's healing, just as he uses surgical procedures and good nutrition. Indeed we must be careful of dictating to God the methods he should employ in the healing of a person's body or personality.

A young woman insisted upon having her baby at home, without a physician, with the help of only God and her husband. It was to be a sort of mystical, religious experience. For the first few hours, labor went well. Then complications set in, and, almost too late, the couple panicked and called an obstetrician who was not happy at being sent for in a crisis rather than at the beginning. This couple's attitude toward using God in place of a physician was a distortion of God's methods. God does not want a Christian to avoid available help, even though he does also divinely intervene in a Christian's life.

The following illustration of C. S. Lewis is one of the best I have encountered.

Imagine three men who go to war. One has the ordinary natural fear of danger that any man has and he subdues it by moral effort and becomes a brave man. Let us suppose that the other two have, as a result of things in their subconsciousness, exaggerated, irrational fears, which no amount of moral effort can do anything about. Now suppose that a psychoanalyst comes along and cures these two: that is, he puts them both back in the position of the first man. Well, it is just then that the psychoanalytical problem is over and the moral problem begins. Because, now that they are cured, these two men might take quite different lines. The first might say, "Thank goodness I've got rid of all those doo-dahs. Now at last I can do what I always wanted to do—my duty to the cause of freedom." But the other might say, "Well, I'm very glad that I now feel moderately cool under fire, but, of course, that doesn't alter the fact that I'm still jolly well determined to look after Number One and let the other chap do the dangerous job whenever I can. Indeed one of the good things about feeling less frightened is that I can now look after myself much more efficiently and can be much cleverer at hiding the fact from the others." Now this difference is a purely moral one and psychoanalysis cannot do anything about it. However much you improve the man's raw material [the various feelings, impulses and so on which his psychological outfit presents him with], you have still got something else: the real, free choice of the man, on the material presented to him, either to put his own advantage first or to put it last. And this free choice is the only thing that morality is concerned with. The bad psychological material is not a sin but a disease. It does not need to be repented of, but to be cured.[5]

Parents who have troubled children face some special problems in terms of social pressure. If the parents are afraid of counseling because it is "weird" or "dangerous," they will project this attitude onto their children. One teenage boy I know begged his parents to allow him to get free counseling at a clinic. But his parents refused because they had had one moderately bad counseling experience years before. Another parent told me to help her son but not to let her know what was wrong. She didn't want to face his problems any further than was absolutely necessary. Another parent who felt that counseling was a "newfangled modern idea" brought his daughter to me with deep, freshly cut slashes on her wrists. A week later he thought she was better and withdrew her from counseling. He said as he left, "She really doesn't have any greater problems than any normal adolescent."

Some parents seem threatened by what will be revealed in the counseling session. Others resent the money spent, and even the child picks up that feeling. As a result some children are taken out of therapy too quickly, usually when the child stops bothering the parent, and sometimes end up back with the counselor a few years later. I suppose this is one of the facets of the helplessness of childhood. Children who hurt often only got help when their behavior irritates their parents. Adults get help and sustain that help until the pain goes away. One small child whom I saw for a few weeks wanted to die and be with her father who had been killed in an automobile accident. Her mother was obviously upset too, and her counseling continued until she had her life back together. But the child's counseling was discontinued "because the mother didn't have time to bring her." She had the money but didn't want to take the hour each week. The last memory I have of Cheri is of holding her while she tried to make me promise that she'd never have to stop coming to me!

Apart from a parent's hangups, the child too at an early age may experience some social stigma from being in counseling. This will depend partly, of course, on the parents' attitudes. A child of a friend visited my office and was intrigued with the games. All through dinner he kept thinking and then saying things like, "I think I really have a problem. I think I should really come and talk to you." It never entered his mind that such visits could be socially unacceptable. But then his parents are broad-minded and have both been in therapy.

In contrast, one seven-year-old I saw loved to come each week and changed rapidly in a very positive way. Yet he didn't want anyone outside his family to know of his visits. Somehow he had picked up the idea that getting counseling was something to hide.

The acceptability of going to a counselor can be shown to a child by the parent who brings him. A nine-year-old boy asked his mother why he was coming to me. Her answer was: "Remember when I was upset and went each week to talk to someone and then felt better?" When the boy said yes, she continued: "Now that you are having problems at school we thought that talking to someone might help you too." Content, the child started six months of profitable counseling. Even now, several years later, this child is accepting toward friends and family when they are upset. He's learned that pain is not something you look down on and that furthermore it can be alleviated.

For an adult himself or for a parent with a child, deciding to seek professional counseling is one thing and knowing how to go about it is another. There are as many personalities and philosophies as there are therapists. The person chosen should have adequate professional training and credentials, but apart from that basic qualification, the philosophy and personality of the counselor is probably of greatest importance. For example, a psychiatrist and a psychologist or a psychologist and a marriage counselor may function more alike than two psychiatrists or two psychologists. Advice from friends about a given counselor can be helpful, except that often friends don't talk about their therapy, and so the job of finding a counselor can be a lonely one. Ministers and doctors often refer, but it is important to be sure that the referral is someone you can relate to, both in philosophy and personality.

I don't necessarily believe that Christians have to go to Christians, but it would be destructive for a Christian to be in therapy with a counselor who continually ridiculed God. It is also important that the relationship have the potential of that previously described. This means that people probably can't get much help from someone they dislike—and that goes for teenagers and children as well!

Usually in a few visits a person will know whether or not the counselor can help him. Then once the right person is found, it is important to have patience; problems which have built up for years will not normally be solved in a few weeks. There are a few such miracles, but they are not usual.

One young man who saw me for a number of months made unusually good progress but then precipitously quit when he started to feel better. He later said that he wanted to prove that he could do it on his own and, beside that, his family was giving him a hard time about being in therapy. Two years later after a suicide attempt he ended up back in my office. What could have been accomplished in a few months two years before later took double that time.

Unfortunately this man's experience with his family occurs far too often. There is therefore probably a delicate balance needed regarding how much to tell one's family and friends. Getting counseling should be something a person should be able to talk about, but one needs an intuitive knowledge of whom he or she can trust to understand. After her mother's death, one woman went to a psychologist for several sessions. She then told an aunt who immediately became greatly upset and told the whole family: "Renee has gone crazy and is seeing a head doctor." Yet when the same woman told her best friend, her response was: "That's great. My sister's doing the same thing, and I think I'd like some help with a few problems. Who are you seeing?"

We are a long way from the day when people only went to therapists when they completely broke down; yet vestiges of that feeling remain. Fortunately the field of psychotherapy has improved, and the combination of psychotherapy, medical treatment, and spiritual help is becoming more common. Along with these changes the average person has become a little more sophisticated about psychological needs and treatment which has enabled more people to get more help.

Rather than being a godless force used to seduce Christians from their faith, counseling can be a God-given, God-used tool to help Christians and non-Christians with emotional problems. The human personality is very delicate and vulnerable; yet the same capacity for destruction is also present for growth. The skillful therapist takes that capacity and uses it to shape and strengthen a good self-image. Sometimes change is slow and almost imperceptible, but perhaps it is then all the more rewarding.

A psychologist in the children's ward at a state hospital had been working for a number of months with an autistic six-year-old boy, Mike. At first, Mike could only relate to inanimate objects like airplanes or boats. Then as time passed by, he became aware of some living things, such as butterflies. And part of the therapy sessions involved chasing countless butterflies, and eventually birds, that were never caught.

Yet Mike was still trapped in an imaginary world of his own. Unable to even accept his own identity, he referred to himself as "Mike," never as "I" or "me." He would say, "Mike wants water" or "Mike is tired." Nor could he relate enough to other human beings to even gain direct eye contact. Instead he would look through them or around them, never at them. His growth in connecting with the reality of the world around him was slow.

Then one day after an exhausting chase around the grounds of the institution, Mike and the therapist collapsed on the grass to rest. As he turned toward the therapist, suddenly Mike's eyes focused directly into the therapist's. He said, "*I* see you in *my* eyes!"[6]

NOTES

1. William Glasser, M.D., *Reality Therapy* (New York: Harper & Row, 1965), chap. 1.

2. George B. Woods and Jerome H. Buckley, eds., *Poetry of the Victorian Period*, rev. ed. (New York: Scott, Foresman & Co., 1955), p. 452.

3. Ibid., p. 453.

4. Rollo May, *The Art of Counseling* (Nashville: Abingdon Press, 1967), p. 119.

5. C. S. Lewis, *Mere Christianity* (New York: Macmillan, 1960), pp. 84–85.

6. Elizabeth Skoglund, *Where Do I Go to Buy Happiness?* (Downers Grove, Ill.: InterVarsity Press, 1972), chap. 3.

CHAPTER 7

————•————

The Responsibility of the
Helping Professions

During the two-month waiting period of a terminal illness in a family, the wife received many phone calls and visits from numerous members of the clergy, mainly from men with whom she was acquainted because of her employment in the community. One afternoon, about three weeks before her husband died, Emily was lying down wondering how she would ever have the energy to get up and finish the day. When the phone rang, it was almost too much to answer it. The voice on the other end belonged to a minister from a church in the next town. Emily had just recently met him, and so she was surprised to hear his voice. "How can I help you?" were his first words. Then, "You sound tired. Maybe I could do your grocery shopping."

Uplifted by this stranger who was willing to help and not just offer words, Emily felt a new surge of strength in her still genuinely tired body. They talked for a while, and this man's love for God and concern for her continued to build her up until, by the end of the conversation, she felt greatly renewed.

A clergyman who was keenly tuned in to the spiritual needs of others had not forgotten that people have emotional and physical needs too. One is reminded of Christ's injunction: "For whosoever shall give you a cup of water to drink in my name, because ye belong to Christ, verily I say unto you, he shall not lose his reward" (Mark 9:41, KJV).

A psychotherapist received a phone call on his day off. Frantically, a young man shouted: "My wife's trying to kill herself, what can I do?" The wife, Marilyn, had been a patient for several weeks and had been making progress. Not wanting to slow down that progress by the further trauma of hospitalization, the therapist got in his car and drove to the couple's home. Once there it took several hours of physically holding her down, administering some medication, and finally talking her back into a desire to live. When she was relatively stabilized and an appointment had been set for the next day, the therapist left, tired and with a sore back. The woman made a recovery without hospitalization because a caring psychotherapist put himself out beyond what was professionally required.

Unfortunately such an extension of oneself is not always possible. Sometimes calls like that hit when there are demands from eight other patients at the same time. Sometimes the person in need is too far away geographically. Often the therapist himself has needs which require an answer of no when everything in him would like to help. There are just so many hours in a day and so much energy that each person has.

Closing the door behind him, a physician sat down at his desk and began to listen to a tired-looking, anxious, middle-aged woman. His office was full of people during what was becoming a flu epidemic, and he could see the lights on his telephone flashing as his receptionist picked up phone messages. Yet something in the shakiness of the woman's voice and the despair in her face made him slow down and really listen. What he heard was a woman who was working too hard at her job and inundated with multiple home problems. He prescribed medication and made an appropriate referral for her youngest son who was on drugs. But most importantly he stayed and listened and then tried to build up her spirits before he sent her on her way.

This physician almost missed a dinner appointment because he went greatly overtime with one patient. But because he recognized the patient's need to be heard and reassured, a woman's pain was lessened. More than that, because of the physician's attitude the patient followed his advice carefully and some permanent results were effected.

Besides the fact that many people in the helping professions often extend themselves and do more than is generally demanded, many also show an intuitive ability to see beyond their own scope and direct people toward a total type of treatment involving all facets of their being. I know psychologists who refer to medical personnel when a psychological problem appears to have a possible physical overlap. Physicians perhaps more frequently refer to counseling those patients who seem to need psychological help. Ministers too are often in a position to refer to counselors and physicians those people who appear to have more than spiritual needs. And, of course, ministers also are sometimes referred to by those who are sensitive enough to perceive spiritual needs in people.

One minister I know counseled with a young couple who had abused their three-year-old girl. The father, in particular, was very angry and yet felt deep guilt. On a spiritual level, the minister was gentle, yet firm and direct. He helped them greatly so that by the time they got psychological help they were in good shape spiritually and very open to further counsel.

In their relationship with the medical profession, many nurses do a superb job of relating to the psychological and even the spiritual needs of their patients.

An elderly woman was called before dawn and notified of her husband's death. The incident occurred during an energy crisis, and so the streets were dark as were the halls of the hospital.

But as she made that painful last visit to her husband's bedside, she noticed that the lights by her husband's room at the end of the corridor were turned on. Some of the gloom disappeared from a very hard moment because a nurse anticipated the psychological impact of darkness at a time of death.

Yet in spite of the many good people in these fields and in contrast to the interrelating of services that does exist, far too often the opposite is true. Marianne is a twenty-seven-year-old woman who came to me as a referral from a priest who wasn't sure what was wrong with her but knew she needed help. At the time I first saw her, her main symptoms were frequent anxiety states accompanied by a general depressiveness. Her nutritional needs were obviously not being met in her high starch-sugar diet, and spiritually, she was guilt-ridden because of her past sex life which had been rather promiscuous. With the help of a psychiatrist who ran medical tests, she was found to be hypoglycemic and was put on a diet along with large doses of vitamins. Then session after session we discussed her feelings of guilt, her desires for a future career in nursing, her friends, and anything else she wanted to talk about. In general she was built up physically, relieved of guilt spiritually through acceptance of God's forgiveness, and encouraged to develop a new estimate of her self-worth through her counseling sessions.

As Marianne became less anxious and less intense, I had the opportunity to question her further about her past history with those in the helping professions. Religiously, she had tried Transcendental Meditation at one extreme and a priest at the other who had told her, "Someday you will find meaning in all this." That statement, by the way, even though it did not show her how to find God, was the most helpful statement anyone made during those years.

She had tried acupuncture and drug therapy. A number of physicians who did not specialize told her she had a nervous stomach and gave her donnatal.

Her psychological quest for help reads like an Edgar Allan Poe horror story: Psychoanalysis in which she analyzed her childhood with no results; shock treatment in a hospital, after which she forgot even what books she had read; group therapy, where people told her she had a lot of faults; individual therapy, where she was told she needed group therapy; and then, to top it all, a psychologist gave her an electric rod which was made to guide cattle in a given direction. The rod was battery run, and every time she was afraid she was supposed to shock herself. The result? Greater fear—even after going from three batteries to one so that the shock was lessened.

In the first place, Marianne may have by some chance just happened to pick out some pretty ineffective people. Certainly not all of them are typical. Yet there's a significance in the fact that this woman sought help in all three areas, psychological, medical, and spiritual, and no one in any of these fields could see beyond his own particular specialty. Furthermore, she went to at least fifteen different people. Here is a classic case of a person with problems in all three areas who has responded favorably from treatment which included the body, mind, and spirit.

Perhaps one of the most important points for a helping professional to remember is that a person is a whole complex being with needs which may extend beyond any one individual's training or gift. A man well trained in Bible exposition once referred a patient to me with the statement: "My gift is teaching the Bible. I'm not good at counseling; so I'm sending this person to you."

Personally I value the medical people and those in the clergy to whom I can refer—or with whom I can consult—because very often indeed a patient's problems are not entirely psychological. Unless I'm tuned in to that fact, I can easily make a misjudgment. For example, just the other day I saw a young woman who has been diagnosed as hypoglycemic, with a very low curve on the Glucose Tolerance Test. After a couple of weeks of good nutrition, she seemed ready to resume a full-time job. "It will be better than staying at home bored," was my reasoning. But in a moment of restraint I decided to call her physician and see if he agreed. He did not, most emphatically! The resulting treatment was a supportive coordination between her physician and myself which will effect more speedy improvement on her part. He and I are blunt with each other, but when we get through talking out our differences, we usually genuinely agree. The patient gets the benefit of our combined help in one total direction. Each of us respects the other's professional expertise—but not to the point where we can't disagree or think for ourselves.

Seeing people as whole persons involves a careful use of all available help. Psychotherapists would do well to be involved more in nutrition and to be aware of new advances in the biochemical treatment of emotional illness.

In the book *Psychodietetics* the astounding statement is made that: "A highly placed American Psychiatric Association official who made an in-depth study of the subject told us privately: 'It borders on malpractice. Not five per cent of practicing psychiatrists—that's a generous estimate—ever ask a patient anything about his medical history."[1]

Furthermore, those in the psychological fields should also be more aware of the spiritual needs of patients, whether they define these needs as spiritual or as psychological. In every person there exists the need for meaning and purpose. While the psychotherapist may not, in some cases, have a definitive answer for this need, he or she can at least acknowledge its validity and encourage the patient to find answers.

One patient told me that a therapist had responded with great hostility to his comments about God, ending with: "Where was God when you became nervous?" Later that same patient said: "All these years that I've been seeking answers, I didn't know what I was looking for. But now I know that it was God."

His statement sounded a little like St. Augustine and Viktor Frankl rolled into one. Yet in a way he was voicing what all of us experience at some level of longing and, hopefully, discovery.

On the other hand, it would be helpful if more ministers were cognizant of the psychological needs of their congregations. Some today are very aware, but too many still spiritualize all needs, and so people continue to feel that if they were better Christians they would indeed be "healthy, wealthy" and in this case, psychologically sound.

Perhaps most pivotal in a patient's life is the family physician, for it is to him that many turn first. It used to be the minister. But often now the physician is confronted with psychological and spiritual problems as well as those that are primarily physical. Thus there is a great opportunity to help and a tremendous need for discernment by the average family physician. Even an understanding on his part of the importance of the psychological and spiritual and a tolerance for new medical advances will put him in a position to help patients and to make intelligent referrals.

Part of knowing that a patient's need may extend beyond any one person's field or personal knowledge and experience is reflected in the ability to admit failure or say, "I don't know."

One man took some pills prescribed by his family physician. He was warned to discontinue the medication if he felt any side affects. After two or three days the man felt increasingly ill and so quit the pills and called his physician. Unfortunately, the physician was out of town, and so the man spoke to the physician's associate who had been involved in the original consultation and thus had agreed to the use of the medication.

"Are you still taking the pills?" questioned the associate.

"No," said the man. "They made me feel worse, and my doctor said to quit if they bothered me."

"Well," returned the associate, "then you have no right even to take my time to talk. Either take the pills or don't bother to call me."

So angry that he could not even respond appropriately, the patient said good-bye and hung up. Even after his own physician apologized profusely for his colleague's actions, the patient left both men, not wanting ever to chance a future encounter with the associate.

All the associate physician had to do was realize that sometimes medication doesn't work as expected and admit that fact to the patient. Because the patient's problems were complicated, a further consultation would have probably been appropriate. But the physician just couldn't admit that possibility—even later when he was confronted by his own colleague!

In contrast, while I was doing some interviewing for this book, I was impressed by the highly trained specialists who would say from time to time, "I don't know." All these men are excellent in their fields, but even in their specialty, they know that they don't have all the answers. Such honesty and self-awareness is refreshing.

Another important part of reaching the whole person is having a basic respect for people. Respect builds self-esteem, and a good self-image helps a person physically, psychologically, and spiritually. If I accept myself, I will be calmer, less prone to physical disease, and more likely to be able to believe that God loves me. An older woman wandered into a medical building looking for help. She spoke little English and was on state aid.

Her family wished that she had never come here from Europe. A kindly person who happened to meet her in the hall of the building went with her into several offices to see if they would treat her. With politeness, and in one case without politeness, she was turned down. At the last office they tried, the doctor agreed to see her, money or no money. But the doctor went one step further; she came out into the waiting room where the woman was sitting alone and said, "I would be most happy to be your doctor if you would like me to." She didn't accept her grudgingly. Rather, she treated her with the same dignity she would have given a paying patient.

Another physician expressed his respect for the frustrated patient who is chronically fatigued from undiagnosed allergies when he wrote:

> This picture is often looked upon as the result of nervous tension and labeled neurosis—which is sometimes the case. More often, based on this diagnosis, the administration of tranquilizers, energizers, pepper-uppers, such as the amphetamines, and thyroid as an empirical basis, leaves the patient more exhausted than before. Psychotherapy may result in a frustrated physician, psychiatrist and patient. The latter then feels inferior, hopeless and depressed. He loses faith both in the healing arts and in himself. He becomes either resigned, a chronic complainer or a pilgrim in search of the holy grail. Some individuals show a remarkable persistence in their search for relief—a truly commendable trait—for sometimes they find it. However, the road may be winding and rough—including many experiences and expenses in the paramedical field. During the process they often develop into saints or devils.[2]

Dignity is important to the human personality; without it a person crumbles. It is not enough just to treat the body or just to instruct the spirit. A Sunday school superintendent organized a good educational program and planned creative, interesting activities, but he showed a complete disregard for the feelings of people. A teenager who volunteered to help with the younger children, and who could have done a good job, was told not to bother because he didn't think they would work well together—he'd rather have an older woman whom he could trust. Thoroughly put down, the girl never volunteered at church again.

In another situation a woman went back to see a physician after a suicide attempt. Later when I talked to the physician he told me not to get too involved because she was "one of those" who had tried suicide and "just wanted attention." No compassion, no respect was shown for her as a human being. No wonder the woman resisted treatment and moved away. This is much in contrast to the physician who looked at a fearful, depressed, sick patient, who certainly was not showing his best side, and said with genuineness: "You're too valuable for us not to help." Or again, how different from the pastor of a large church who sat with a depressed woman in the hospital at two in the morning, waiting until she went to sleep.

Even psychotherapists, who should be very interested in the feelings of their patients since respect is ego building, sometimes seem unconscious of this need. One way in which this attitude is shown is in the tendency among some to be label happy. Psychological labels often have dubious accuracy and frequently do not help in treatment. I well remember one boy whom I saw when I was a beginning counselor. I was doing fine with him until a colleague-friend told me that the boy was schizophrenic and that maybe I should refer him. After much consideration and also consultation with people whose opinions I respected more than the first colleague, I decided that the boy was indeed not schizophrenic. Furthermore, our relationship and progress were both good, so why quit? Today he is living a normal life, both socially and professionally, but a label nearly stopped a good counseling situation. More than that, the label in this boy's case, was thrown by a person who had hardly any facts about the case. That's like the court psychiatrist who labeled a man a latent homosexual and a schizophrenic—neither of which he was—after one interview. Or the patient who came to me in a panic when a psychotherapist had labeled her manic-depressive after a ten-minute interview. Here, too, the diagnosis was inaccurate. Even less-threatening labels like neurasthenia are carelessly thrown around and can cause injury. The label neurasthenia has frequently been used in cases which later proved to be hypoglycemia or some other metabolic disorder. Thus that particular label, along with the term *nervous breakdown*, has become a catchall, meaningless diagnosis.

Labels are often important for treatment, especially when biochemical factors are involved and medication and diet are used. But quick, clever labeling can destroy a person's sense of worth very quickly in some cases. The same is true for an overuse of hospitalization. If a person is really dangerous to himself or others, he may need hospitalization. Otherwise psychiatric hospitalization tends to do more harm than good and occasionally seems to become a period of holding a person rather than treating him or her.

One man described his hospitalization as a period of "walking around in a drugged stupor" and feeling "totally isolated" from other people because no visitors except his wife were allowed. He only saw his physician about two or three brief times during the three weeks he spent in the hospital. He wanted to talk, to get some feelings of relatedness to other people, but instead he played head games with the hospital staff until he finally convinced them that he was well enough to go home.

At times hospitalization is a copout for a therapist who wants to get a good night's sleep. I and other people I know in this field have at times taken 4 A.M. phone calls and talked people down from suicide. This is harder on the therapist than hospitalization, but easier on the patient. Yet at times like that, just this sort of giving of oneself to a person in trouble raises the patient's sense of self-worth. "If I'm worth someone else's time in the middle of the night, then I must be of value."

In addition to all of these concepts which have a unifying effect among the helping professions is the need to keep as current as possible in new research and treatment. To keep up completely with all that is being discovered or experimented with in these fields is impossible. A medical specialist probably cannot ever familiarize himself with all the material in his own field, much less others. Yet we need at least an openness to new ideas. The physician who said to me, "I don't believe in hypoglycemia," and then asked me very basic questions about it had kept neither an openness of mind regarding the subject nor a breadth of knowledge about a subject which is directly in his own field. At least be willing to learn, to question, to change. Only insecure persons cannot expand and develop, and in the helping professions insecurity can hurt patients.

One physician whom I interviewed makes a point of hearing lectures and reading material which touch on issues new to him. This takes hours of time—more than one could reasonably expect of him—and yet it has developed a physician who has a great breadth of knowledge and an awareness of new innovations in medicine.

In a day when specialization isolates and people have become numbers in a computer, the need is even greater for treatment of the complete person. Perhaps more than any other psychiatrist I have encountered, Viktor Frankl magnificently states this need.

> When the surgeon has completed an amputation, he takes off his rubber gloves and appears to have done his duty as a physician. But if the patient then commits suicide because he cannot bear living as a cripple—of what use has the surgical therapy been? Is it not also part of the physician's work to do something about the patient's attitude toward the pain of surgery or the handicap that results from it? Is it not the physician's right and duty to treat the patient's attitude toward his illness . . .[3]

Then continuing:

> The night before her leg was to be amputated for tuberculosis of the bone, another patient wrote a letter to a friend hinting at thoughts of suicide. The letter was intercepted and fell into the hands of a doctor in the surgical ward where this patient lay. The doctor lost no time, but found a pretext for a talk with the woman. In a few appropriate words he too pointed out to the patient that human life would be a very

poor thing indeed if the loss of a leg actually involved depriving it of all meaning. Such a loss could at most make the life of an ant purposeless since it would no longer be able to achieve the goal set for it by the ant community—namely running around on all six legs and being useful. For a human being it must be different. The young doctor's chat with the woman, couched rather in the style of a Socratic dialogue, did not fail to take effect. His senior surgeon, who undertook the amputation next morning, does not know to this day that in spite of the successful operation this patient almost ended up on his autopsy table.[4]

Furthermore, in relating psychotherapy and religion, Frankl says:

> Religion provides man with a spiritual anchor, with a feeling of security such as he can find nowhere else. But to our surprise, psychotherapy can produce an analogous, unintended side effect. For although the psychotherapist is not concerned with helping his patient to achieve a capacity for faith, in certain felicitous cases the patient regains his capacity for faith.[5]

In treating a person as a complete being with overlapping needs, the professional functions at an optimum level of efficiency. In the end, he himself comes out way ahead because his own self-worth is higher as a result of his professional success. As the psychiatrist Dubois once said of the medical professions: "Of course one can manage without all that and still be a doctor, but in that case one should realize that the only thing that makes us different from a veterinarian is the clientele."

NOTES

1. Dr. E. Cheraskin and Dr. W. M. Ringsdorf, Jr., with Arline Brecher, *Psychodietetics* (New York: Stein & Day, 1974), p. 97.

2. Granville F. Knight, M.D., *Journal of Applied Nutrition* 16 (1963): 118.

3. Viktor E. Frankl, M.D., *The Doctor and the Soul* (New York: Bantam, 1967), p. 228.

4. Ibid., pp. 229–30.

5. Ibid., p. xiv.